Louis Armstrong
ORIGINAL KEYS FOR SINGERS

Cover photo: Photofest

Thanks to the LOUIS ARMSTRONG EDUCATIONAL FOUNDATION, INC., Oscar Cohen, and Phoebe Jacobs

ISBN 978-1-4234-6587-4

HAL•LEONARD®
CORPORATION
7777 W. BLUEMOUND RD. P.O. BOX 13819 MILWAUKEE, WI 53213

Visit Hal Leonard Online at
www.halleonard.com

AIN'T MISBEHAVIN'

Words by ANDY RAZAF
Music by THOMAS "FATS" WALLER
and HARRY BROOKS

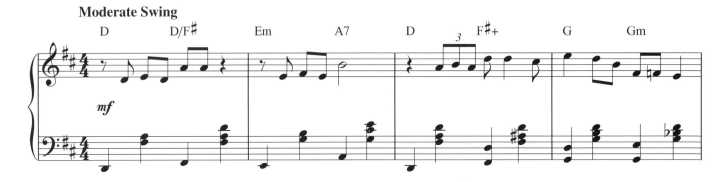

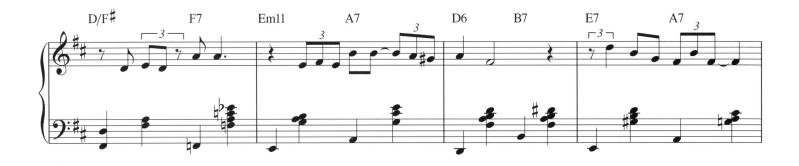

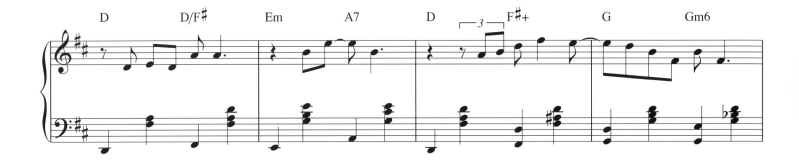

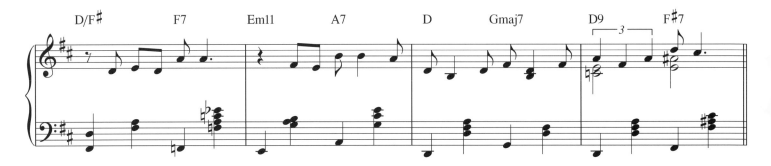

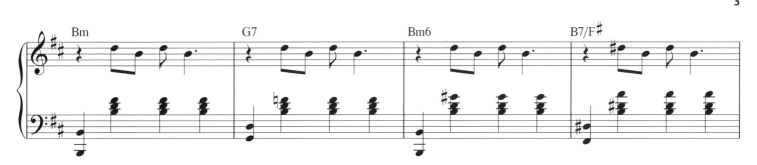

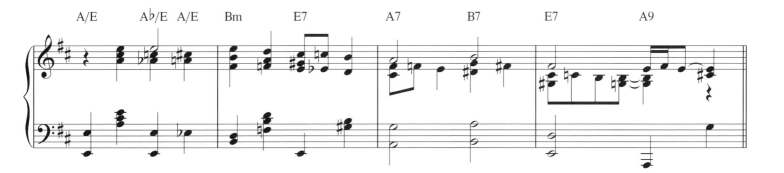

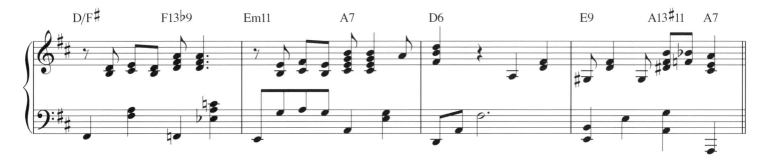

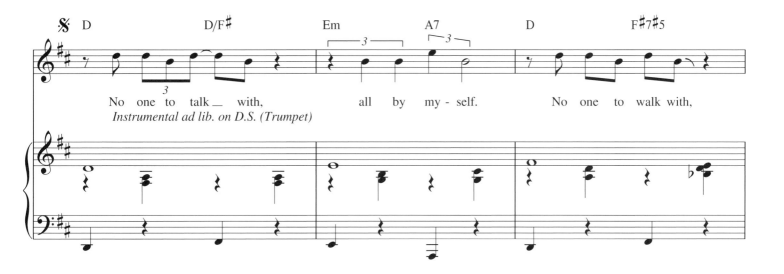

No one to talk__ with, all by my‑self. No one to walk with,

Instrumental ad lib. on D.S. (Trumpet)

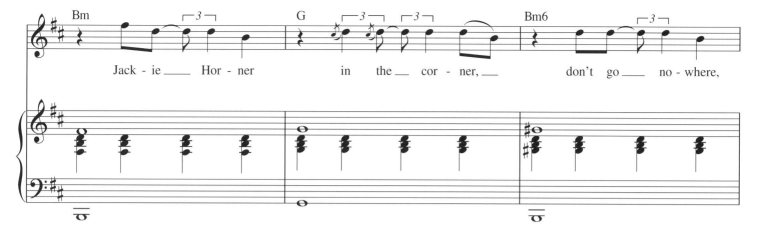

D.S. al Coda

Ain't mis-be-hav-in', sav-in' all my love for you.

Stop-time

rit.

BASIN STREET BLUES

Words and Music by
SPENCER WILLIAMS

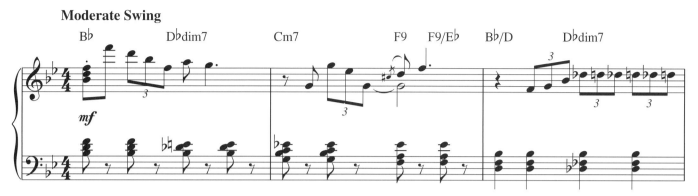

1. *Instrumental ad lib. (trumpet)*
2. ___ Ba - sin Street ___
3. *Instrumental ad lib. (piano)*

is the street where the folks, they all meet,

in New ___ Or - leans, ___ in the land _____ of dreams. Ba -

dat, daz - is - bose - oh, - boo - doot - duz - bez - diz - wall - ya. Mmm, yeah, _____

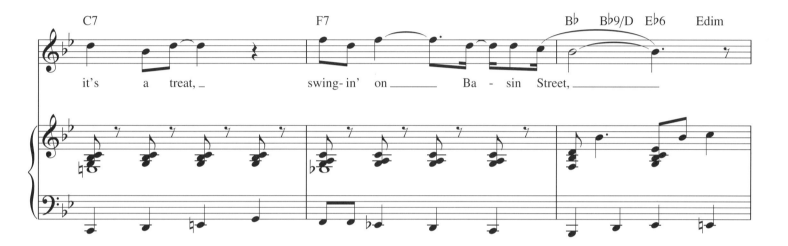

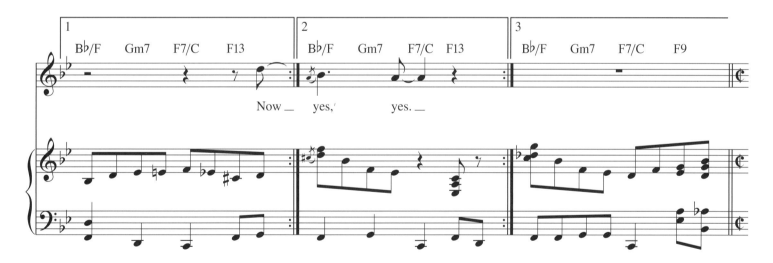

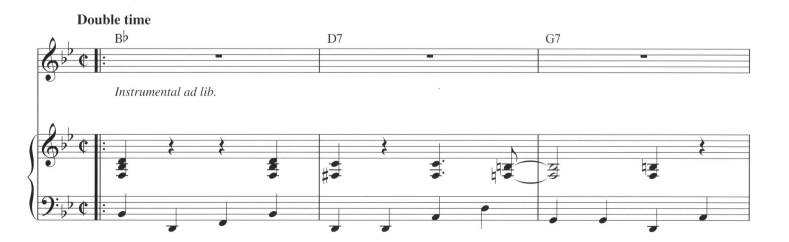

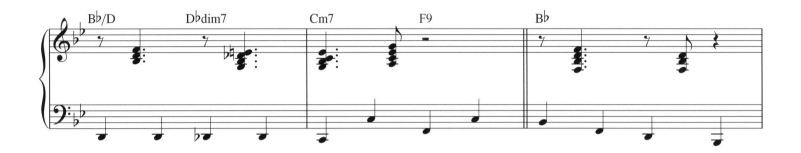

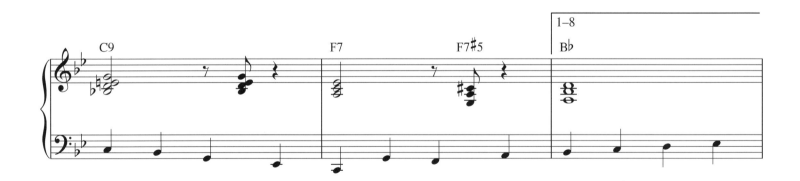

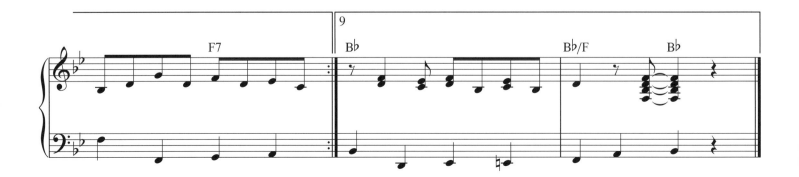

CABARET

Words by FRED EBB
Music by JOHN KANDER

Moderate Swing

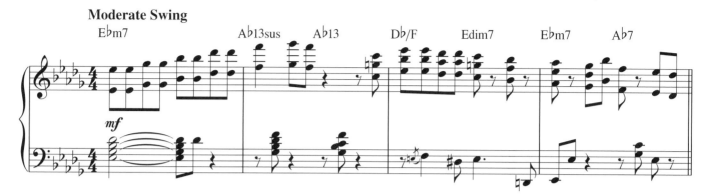

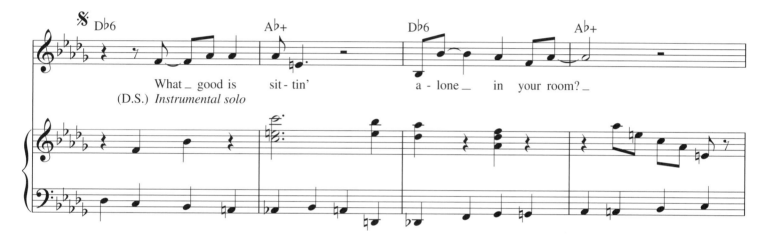

What good is sit-tin' a-lone in your room?
(D.S.) Instrumental solo

Come hear the mus-ic play, yes.

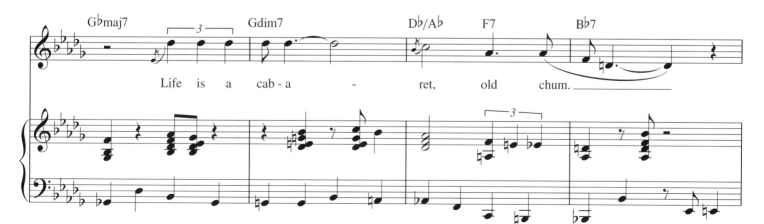

Life is a cab-a - ret, old chum.

Come _ to the cab-a - ret. _____

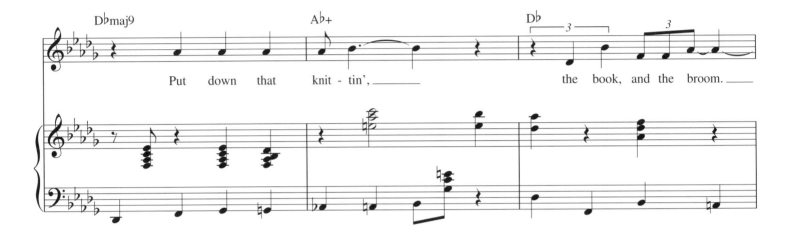

Put down that knit - tin', _____ the book, and the broom. _____

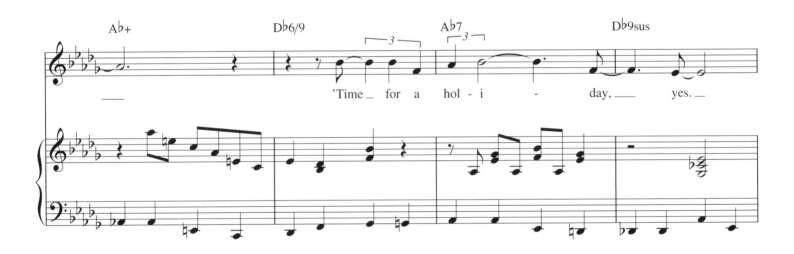

_____ 'Time _ for a hol - i - day, _____ yes. _____

Life is a cab-a - ret, old _ chum, _____

To Coda ⊕

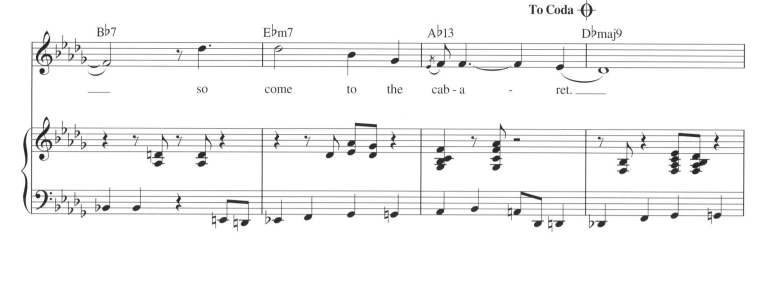

so come to the cab - a - ret.

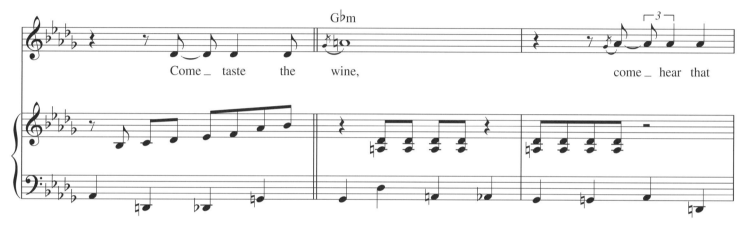

Come _ taste the wine, come _ hear that

band. Yes, it's time for cel - e - brat - in'.

Right this way, _ your ta - ble's wait - in'. No use per - mit - tin' some _

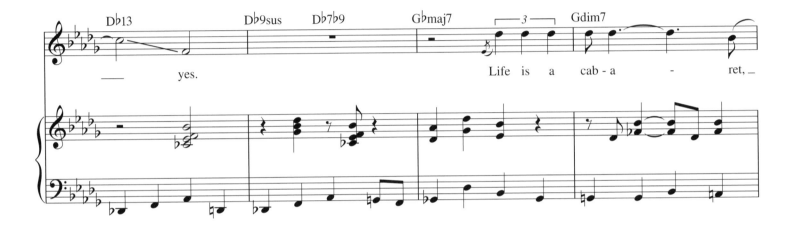

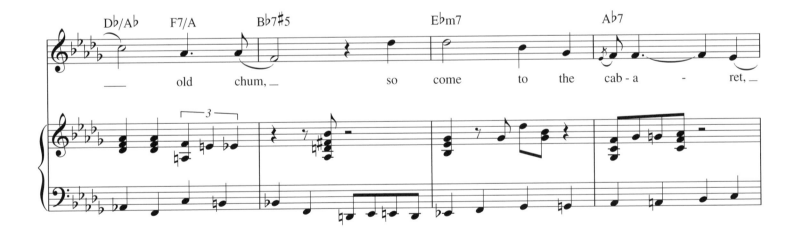

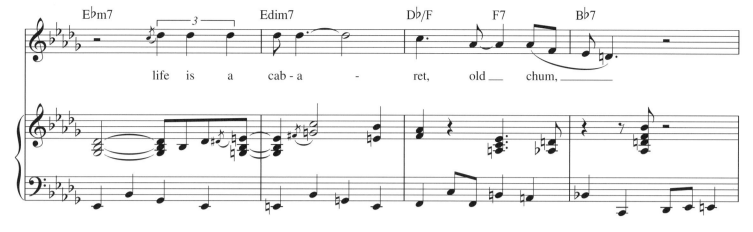

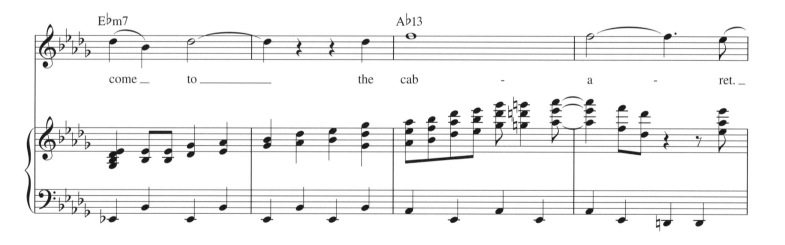

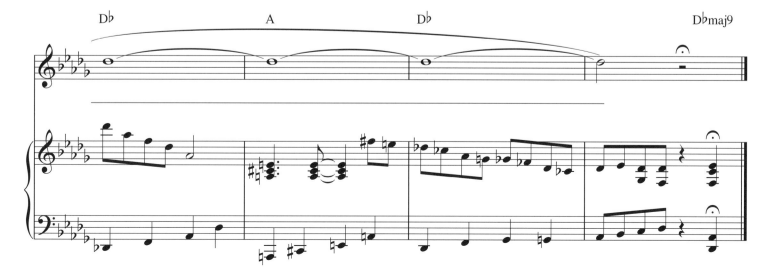

DO YOU KNOW WHAT IT MEANS TO MISS NEW ORLEANS

Written by EDDIE De LANGE
and LOUIS ALTER

Moderate Swing

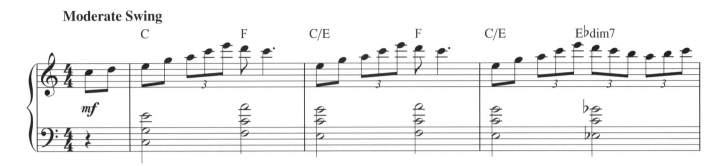

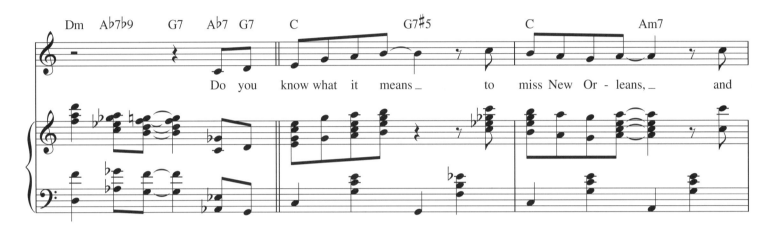

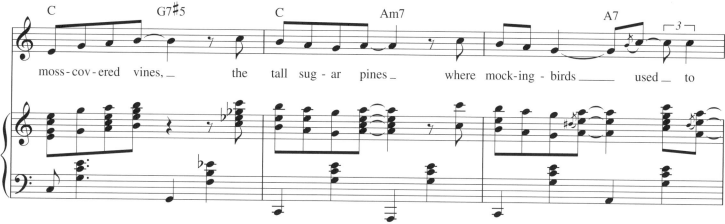

moss-cov-ered vines, _ the tall sug-ar pines _ where mock-ing-birds _____ used _ to

sing. And I'd like to see ___ the laz-y Mis-sis-sip-pi a

hur-ry-in' in-to spring. ___ Oh, __ the Mar - di Gras, _

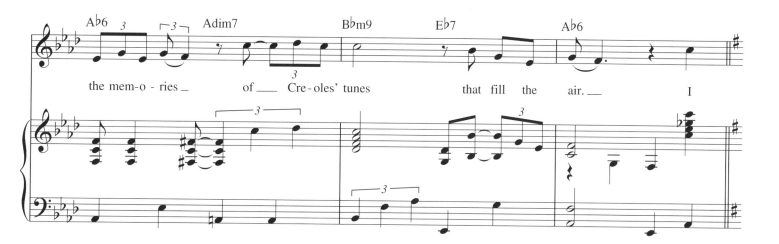

the mem-o-ries _ of ___ Cre-oles' tunes that fill the air. __ I

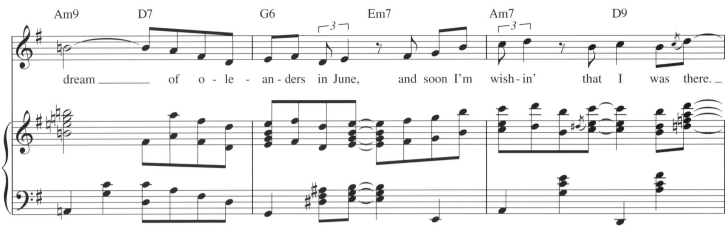

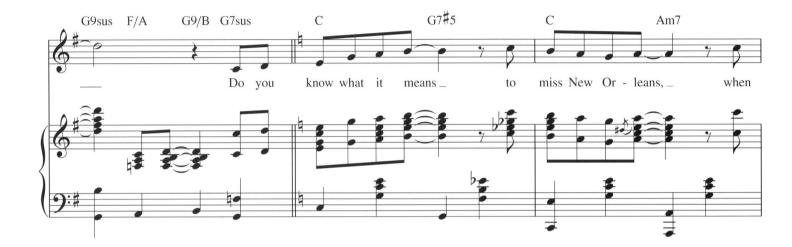

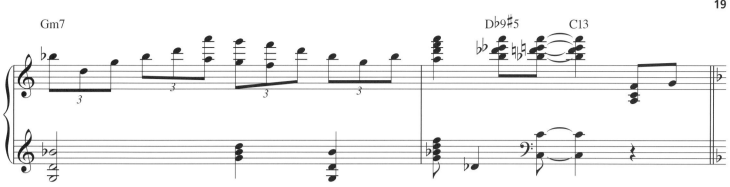

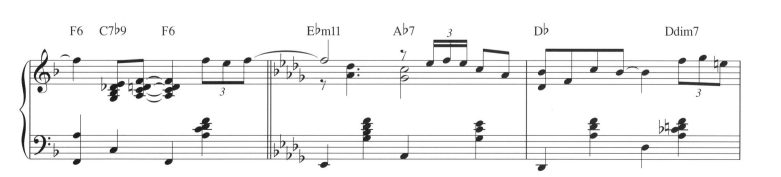

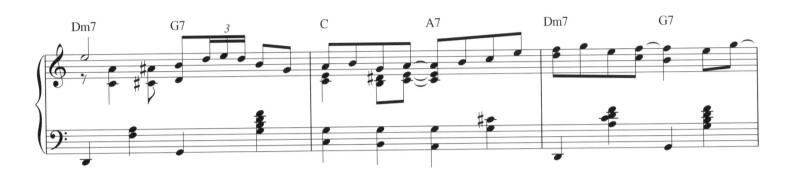

DREAM A LITTLE DREAM OF ME

Words by GUS KAHN
Music by WILBUR SCHWANDT
and FABIAN ANDREE

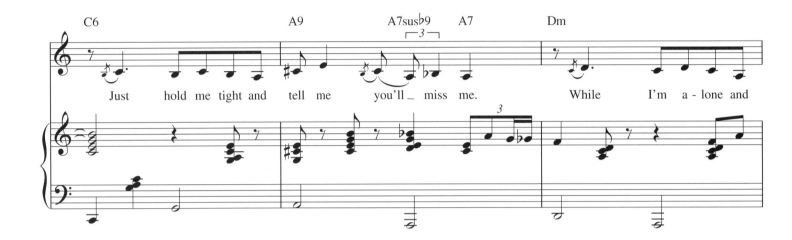

ooh, yeah. But in your dreams, what-ev-er they be,

leave your wor-ries be-hind you. But in your dreams, what-ev-er they be, you've got-ta

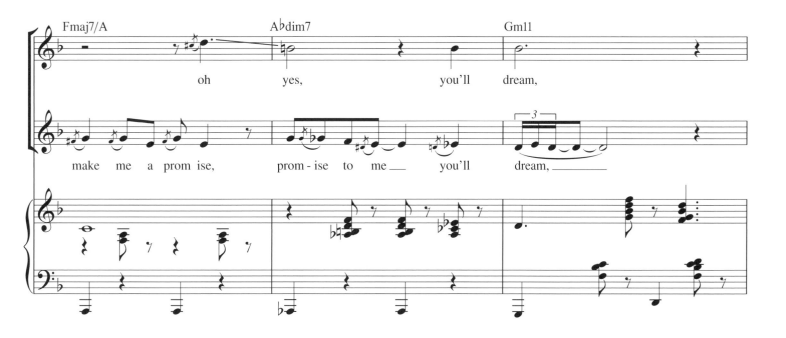

oh yes, you'll dream,

make me a prom ise, prom-ise to me you'll dream,

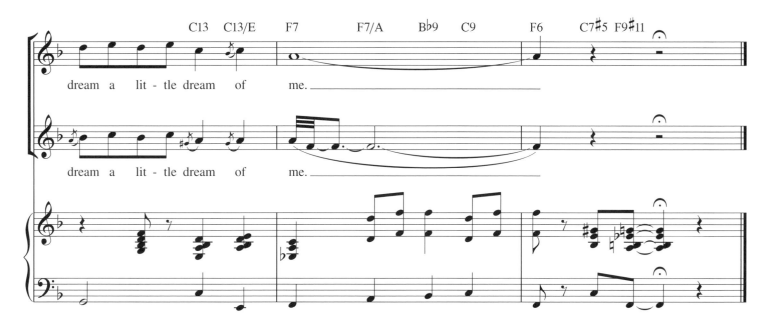

dream a lit-tle dream of me.

dream a lit-tle dream of me.

GEORGIA ON MY MIND

Words by STUART GORRELL
Music by HOAGY CARMICHAEL

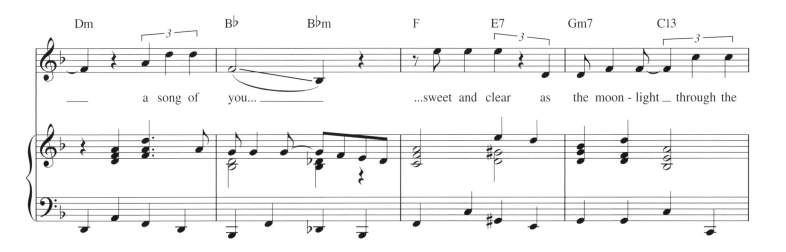

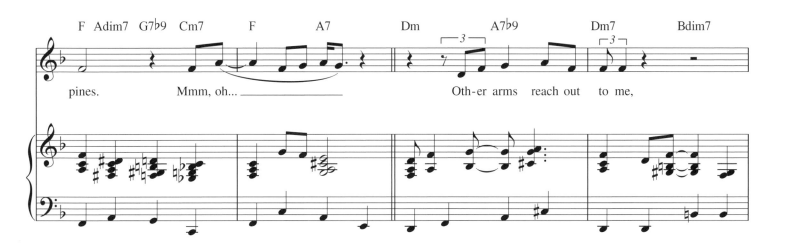

oth-er dames smiles ___ ten-der-ly, mmm, ___ still in peace-ful

___ dreams ___ I see ___ the road it leads back ___ to you, mmm, whoa. ___

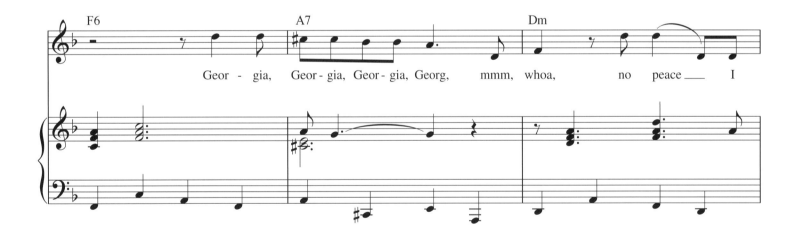

Geor-gia, Geor-gia, Geor-gia, Georg, mmm, whoa, no peace ___ I

find, ___ babe. Just an old sweet song ___ keep Geor-gia on ___ my

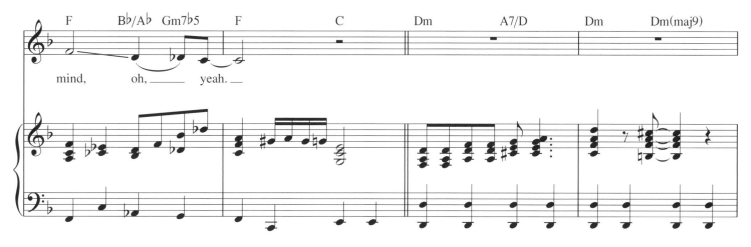

mind, oh, _____ yeah. _____

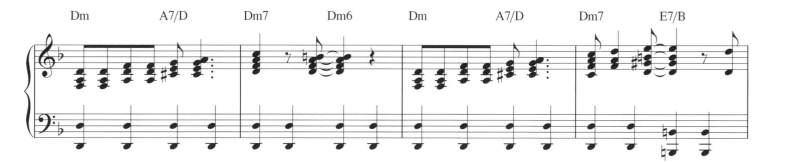

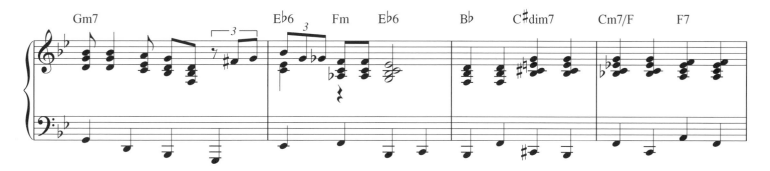

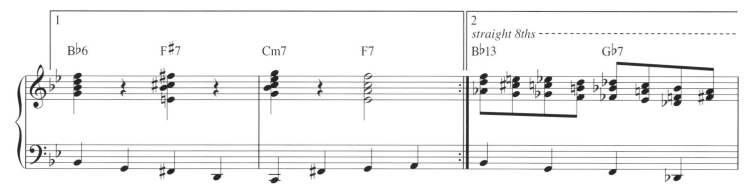

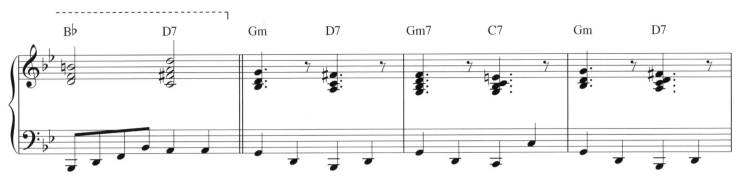

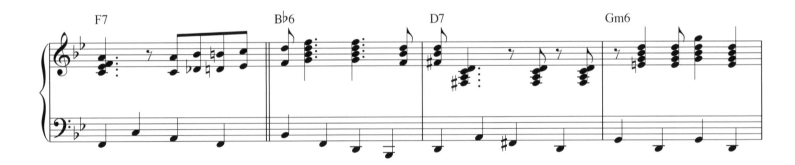
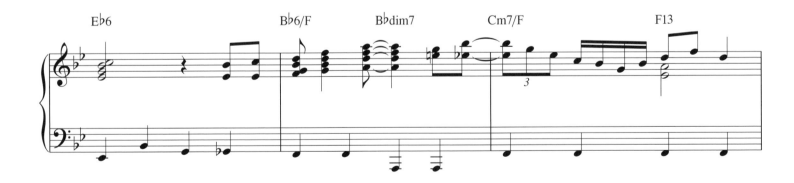
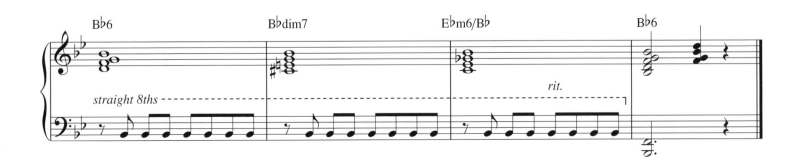

HELLO, DOLLY!

Music and Lyric by
JERRY HERMAN

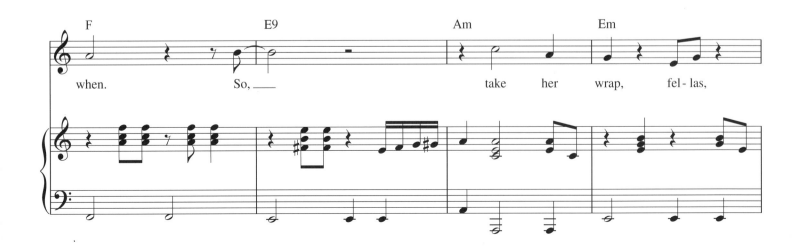

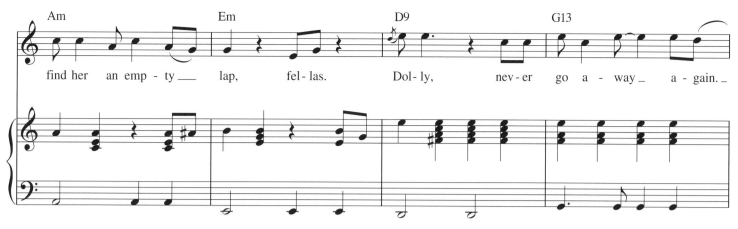

find her an emp- ty ___ lap, fel- las. Dol- ly, nev- er go a- way ___ a- gain. ___

I ___ feel the

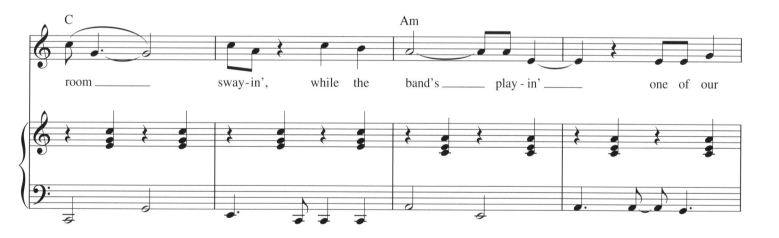

room ___ sway- in', while the band's ___ play- in' ___ one of our

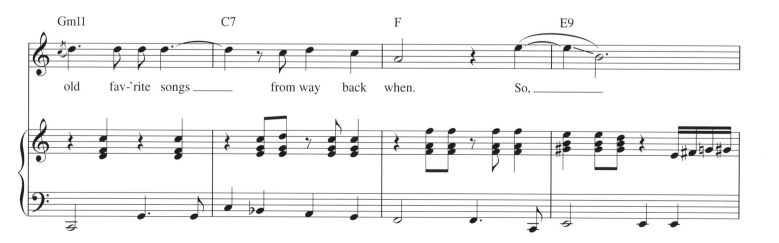

old fav-'rite songs ___ from way back when. So, ___

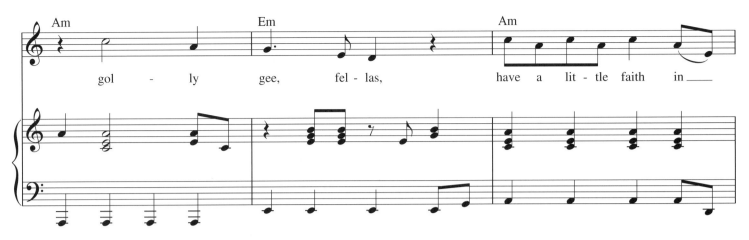

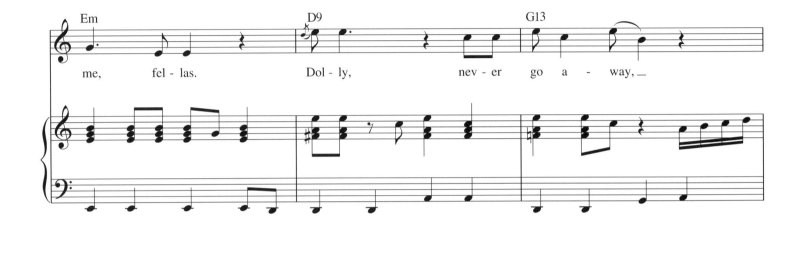

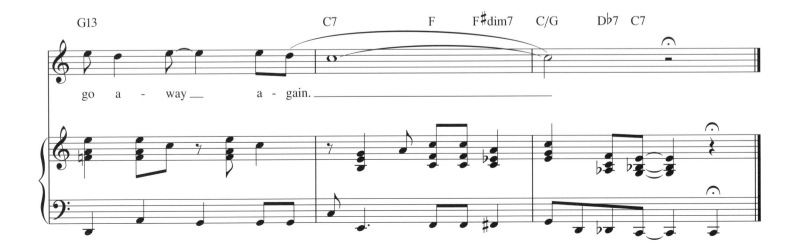

A KISS TO BUILD A DREAM ON

Words and Music by BERT KALMAR,
HARRY RUBY and OSCAR HAMMERSTEIN II

Give me a kiss to build a dream on, and my i-mag-i-na-tion will thrive up-on that kiss. Mmm, sweet-heart, I ask no more than this: ___ a kiss to build a dream on. ___

Instruemental ad lib. on D.S. (Trumpet)

Give me a kiss be-fore you leave me, and my i-mag-i-

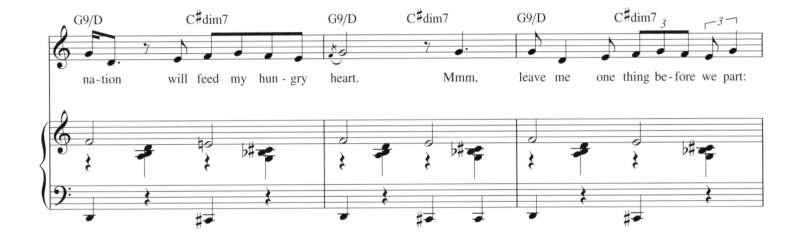

na-tion will feed my hun-gry heart. Mmm, leave me one thing be-fore we part:

a kiss to build a dream on. ___ When I'm a-lone _
(Vocal re-enters on D.S.)

___ with my fan-cies, ___ I'll ___ be with you, ___

38

MACK THE KNIFE

English Words by MARC BLITZSTEIN
Original German Words by BERT BRECHT
Music by KURT WEILL

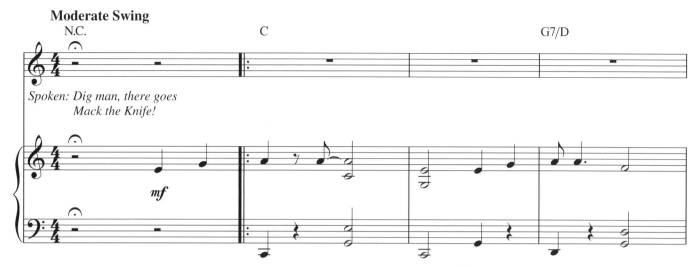

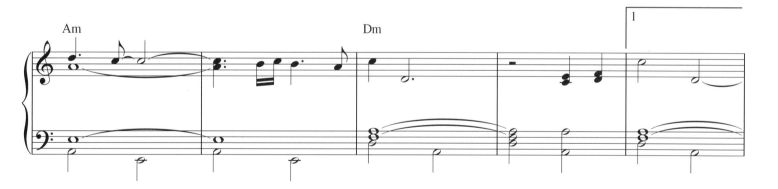

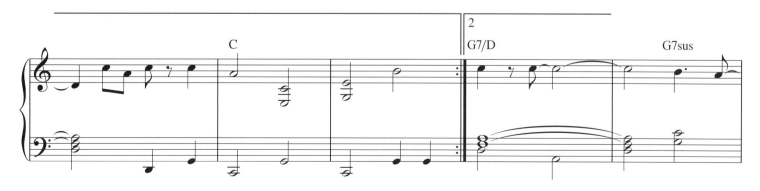

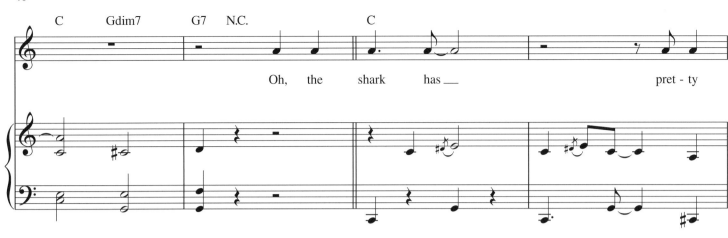

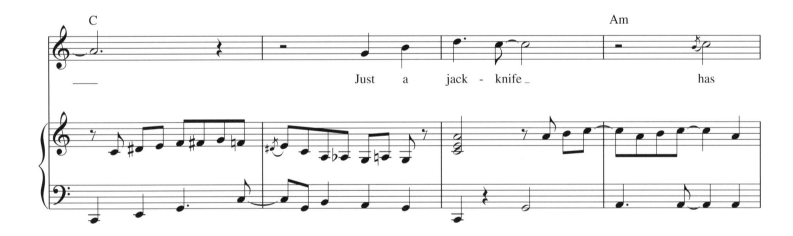

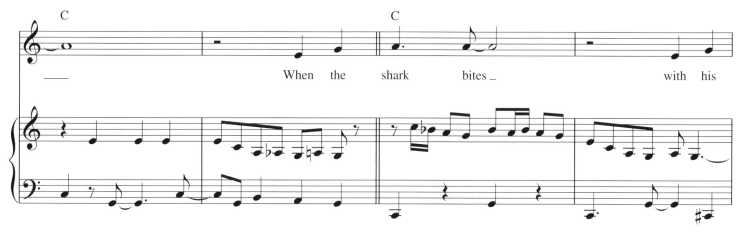

When the shark bites ____ with his

teeth, ___ dear, _ scar - let ____ bil-lows start to spread. _

Fan - cy gloves, though, _____ wears _ Mac-

heath, dear, _____ so there's not a trace, _____ mmm, ___ of

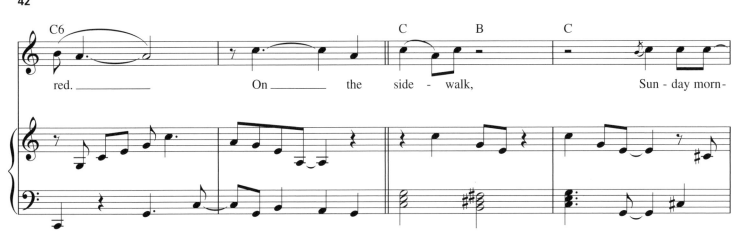

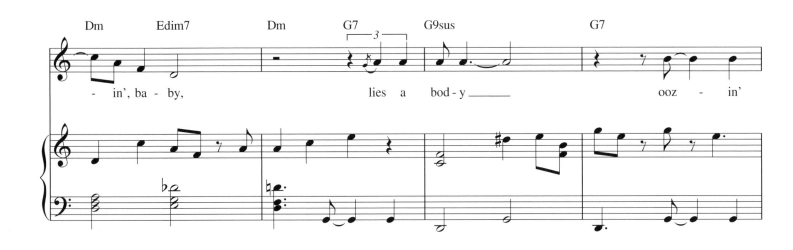

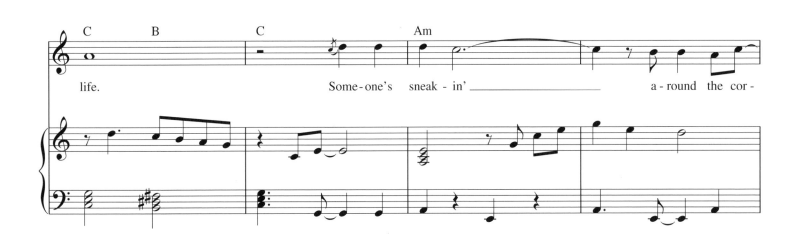

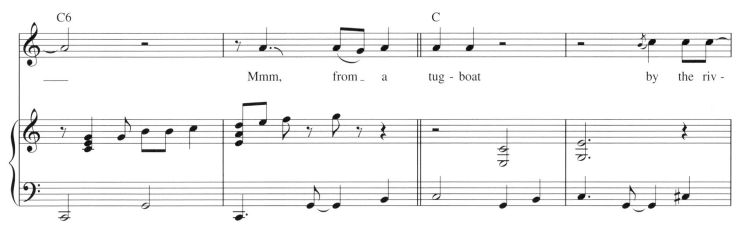

Mmm, from a tug-boat by the riv-

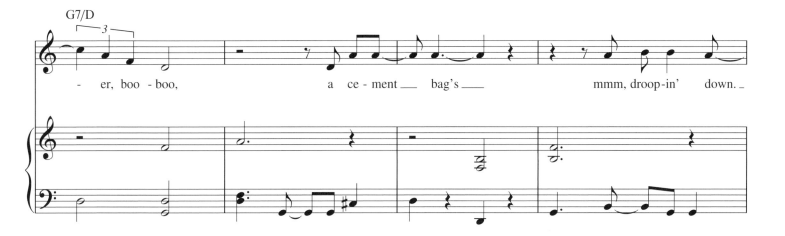

-er, boo-boo, a ce-ment bag's mmm, droop-in' down.

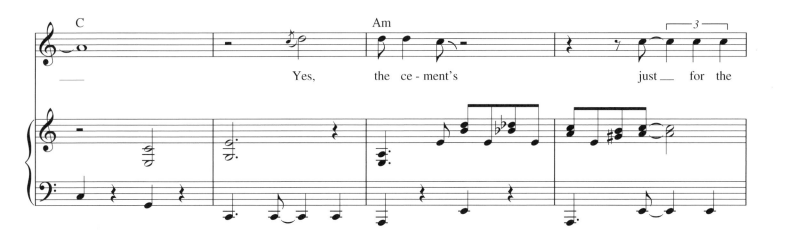

Yes, the ce-ment's just for the

weight, dear. 'Bet you Mac-heath's back in town.

Look - a here, Lou - ie Mil - ler   dis - ap -

peared, dear, _   af - ter _ draw - ing _   out his cash, _

_   and Mac - heath spends _   like a sail -

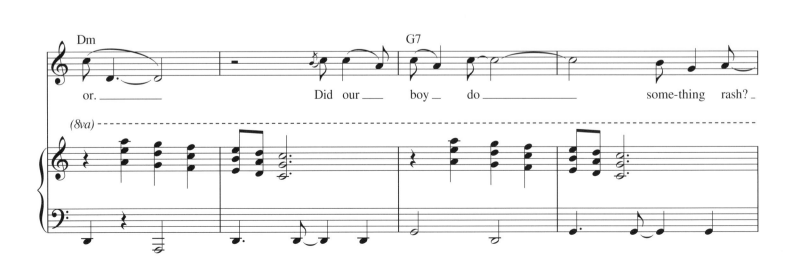

or. _   Did our _ boy _ do _   some - thing rash? _

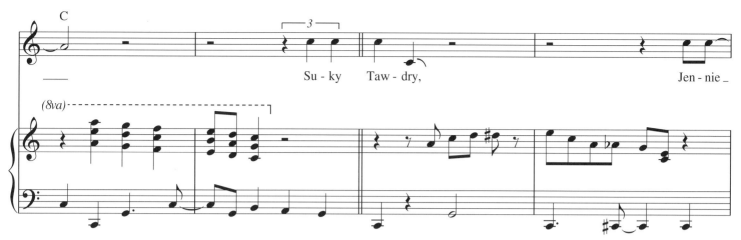

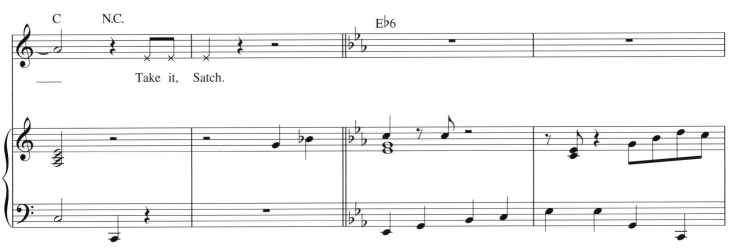

Take it, Satch.

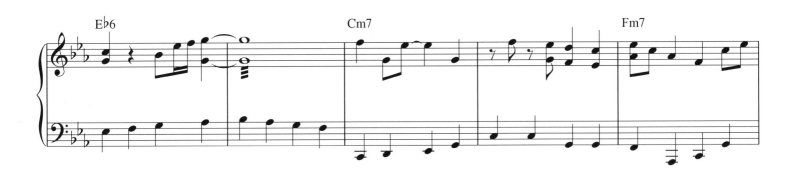

MAKIN' WHOOPEE!

Lyrics by GUS KAHN
Music by WALTER DONALDSON

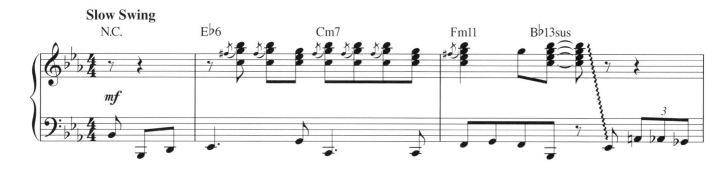

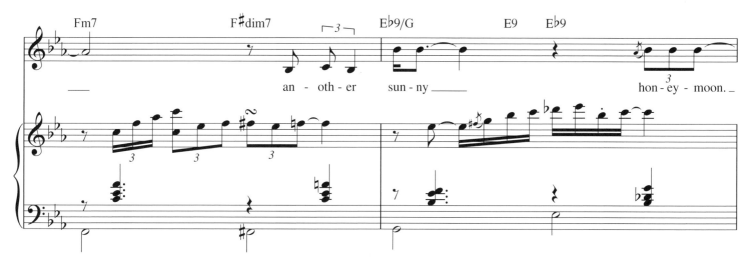

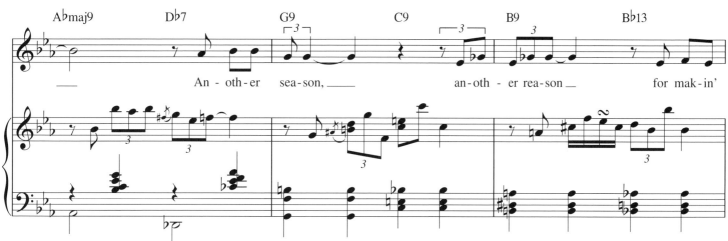

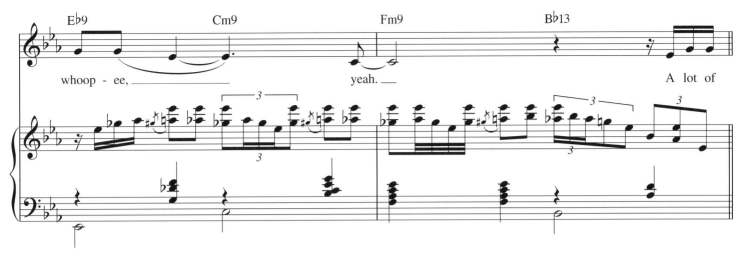

whoop - ee, _____ _____ yeah. ___ A lot of

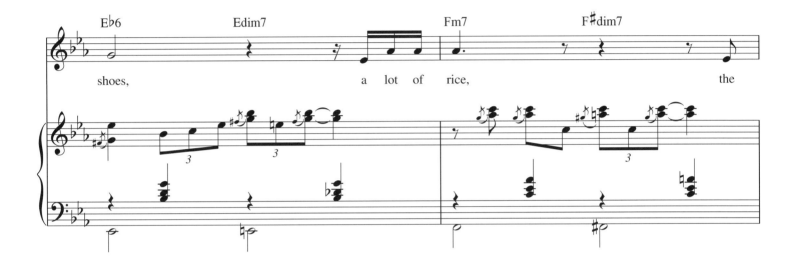

shoes, a lot of rice, the

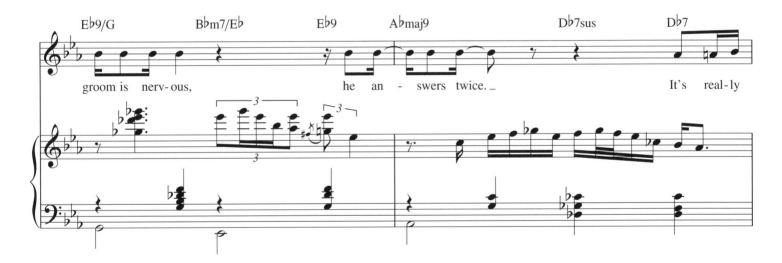

groom is nerv-ous, he an - swers twice. ___ It's real-ly

kill - in' _____ that he's ___ so will - in' to make ___

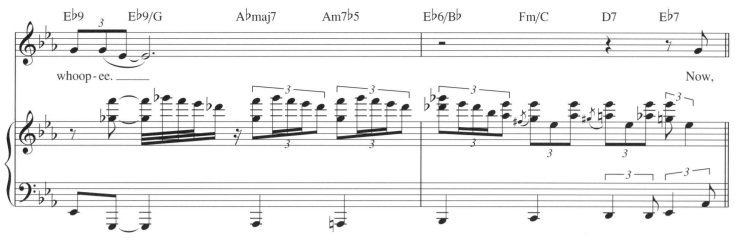

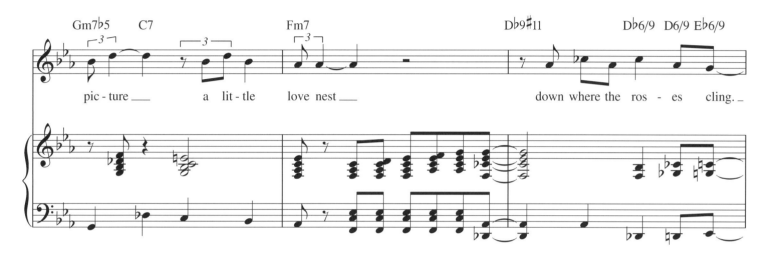

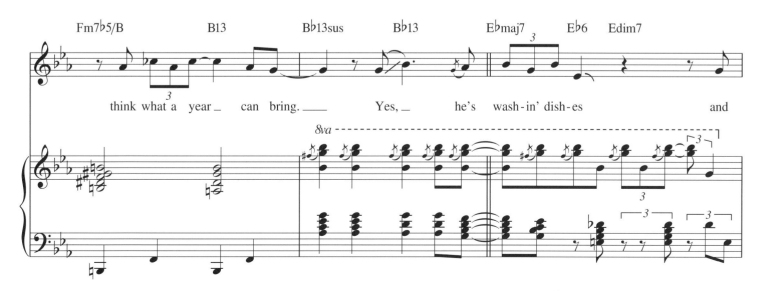

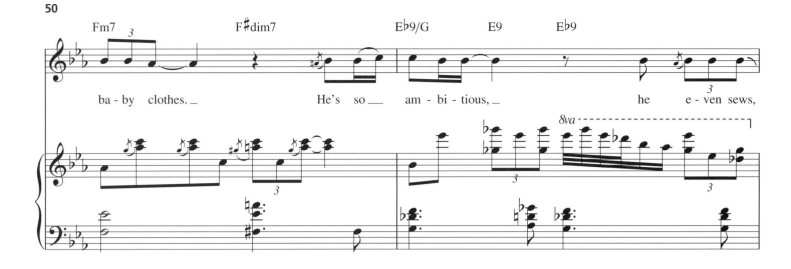

ba - by clothes. ___ He's so ___ am - bi - tious, ___ he e - ven sews,

but don't for - get, folks, that's what you get, folks, for mak - in'

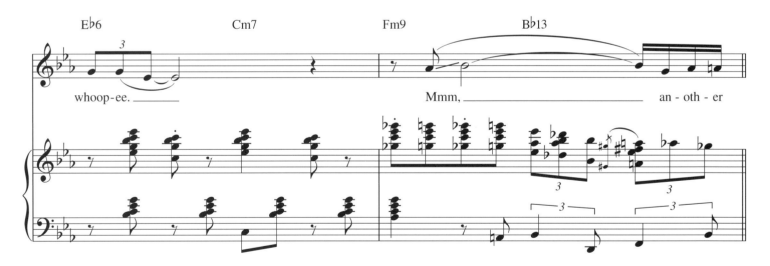

whoop-ee. ___ Mmm, ___ an - oth - er

year, um, may-be less... "What's this I hear?" Well, can't you guess? ___

She feels ne-glect-ed, and he's _ sus - pect-ed of mak-in'

whoop - ee. Yes, _____ she sits a-lone most __ ev'ry

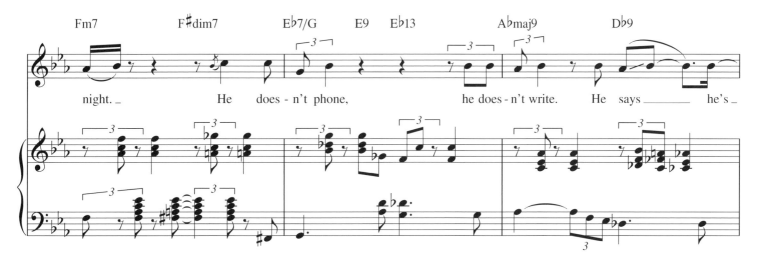

night. _ He does - n't phone, he does - n't write. He says _____ he's _

__ bus - y, but she says, _ "Is he?" He's _ mak -

in' whoop-ee. ___ Now, he does-n't ___ make ___ much ___

mon-ey, on - ly five thou-sand per. ___

Some judge who thinks he's fun-ny says he'll pay ___ six ___

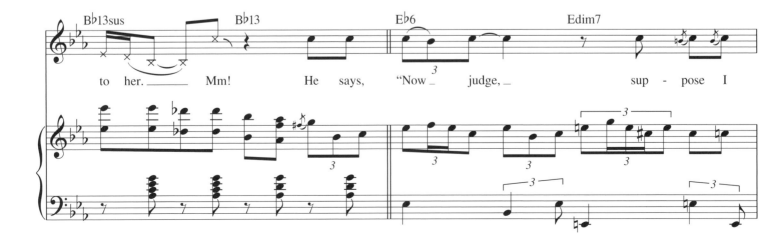

to her. ___ Mm! He says, "Now ___ judge, ___ sup - pose I

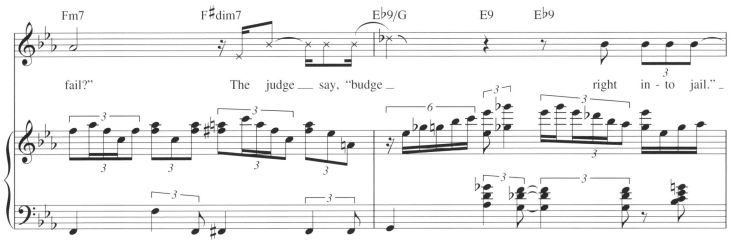

Fm7　F#dim7　Eb9/G　E9　Eb9

fail?"　The judge ___ say, "budge ___ right in - to jail." ___

Abmaj9　Db13　G13　C7　B13#11　Bb13

___ You'd bet-ter keep her, mmm, I ___ think it's cheap-er than mak-in'

Eb6　Gm7b5　C13　Fm7　F#dim7　B13

whoop-ee. ___ Yes, ___ yeah, you bet-ter keep her, ___ dad-dy, I think it's

Bb13sus　Bb13b9　Eb7　Eb7/G　Ab13　Adim7　Eb/Bb　E6/9#11　Eb6/9

cheap-er ___ than mak-in' whoop-ee. ___

MAME

Music and Lyric by
JERRY HERMAN

You _ coax the blues right out _ of the horn, Mame. _
Instrumental ad lib. on D.S. (Trombone)
Mame. _

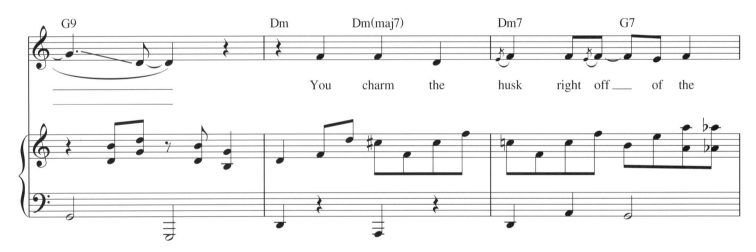

You charm the husk right off _ of the

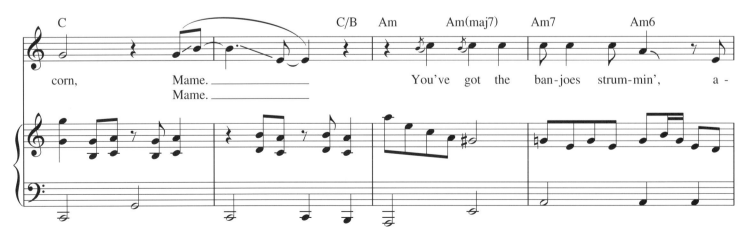

corn, Mame. _____
Mame. _____
You've got the ban-joes strum-min', a-

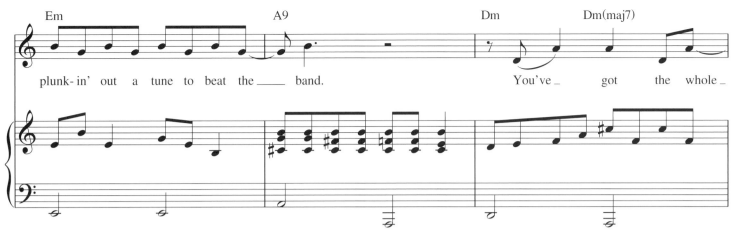

plunk-in' out a tune to beat the _____ band. You've _ got the whole _

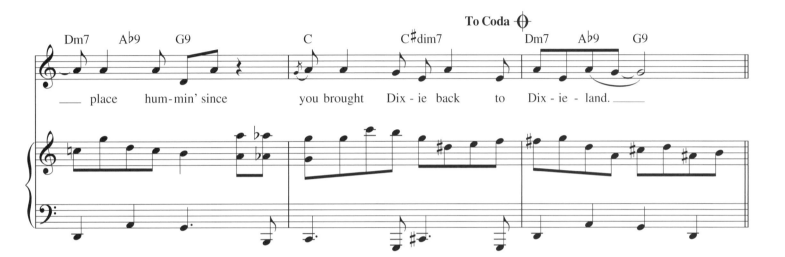

To Coda ⊕

_____ place hum-min' since you brought Dix - ie back to Dix - ie - land. _____

You make your Lou - ie feel _ like a king, Mame. _____

You make the world _ we liv - in' in swing, _ Mame. _

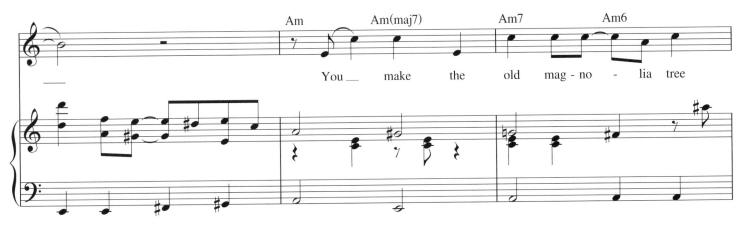

You make the old mag-no-lia tree

blos-som at the men-tion of your name. Your spec-ial

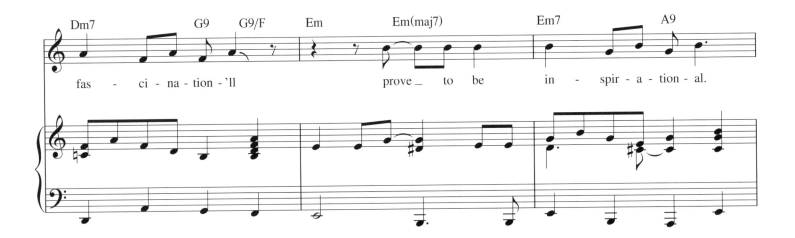

fas-ci-na-tion-'ll prove to be in-spir-a-tion-al.

D.S. al Coda

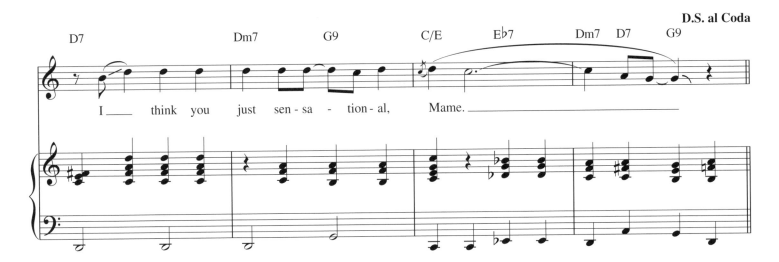

I think you just sen-sa-tion-al, Mame.

CODA

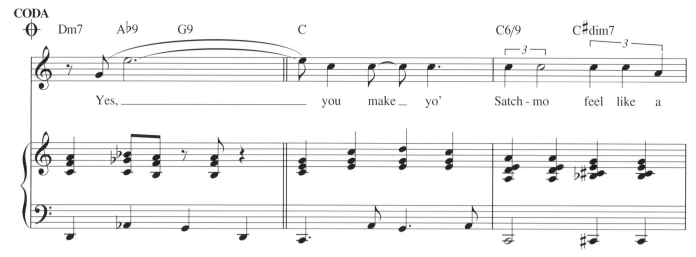

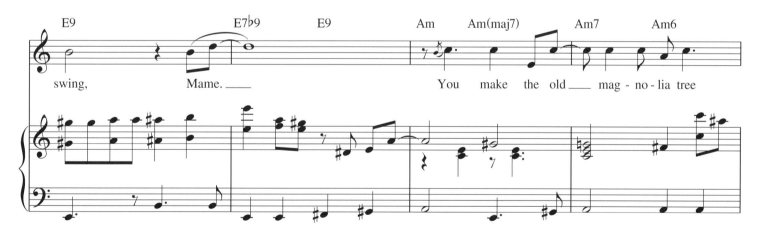

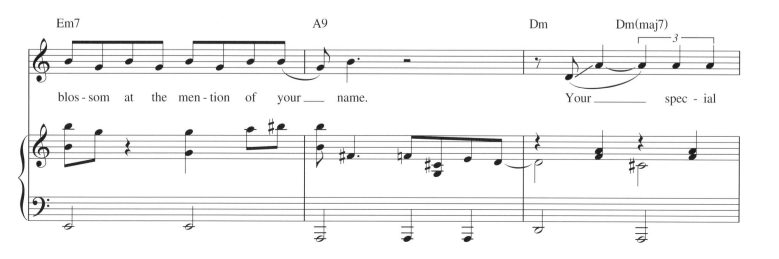

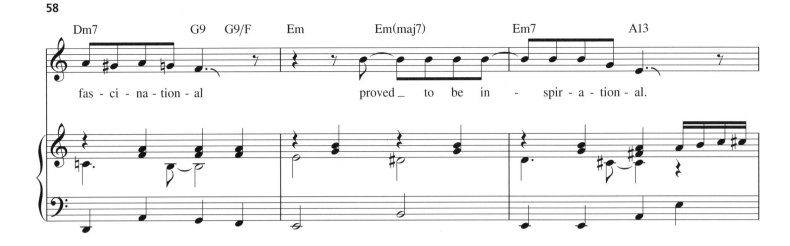

fas - ci - na - tion - al proved _ to be in - spir - a - tion - al.

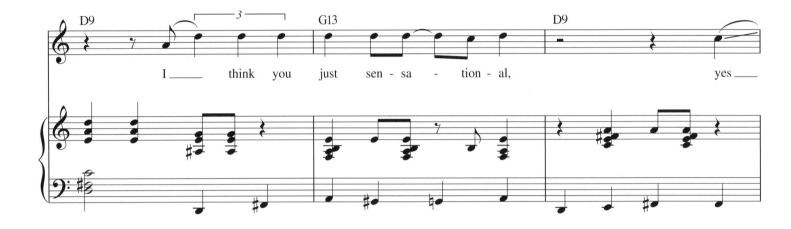

I _____ think you just sen - sa - tion - al, yes _____

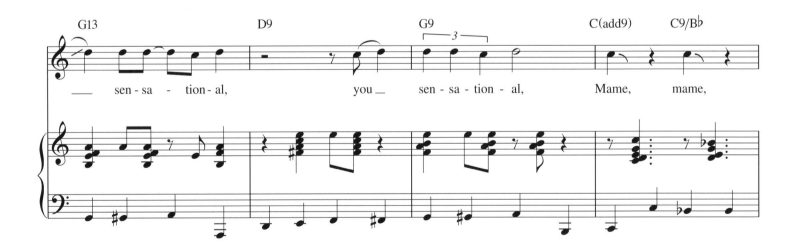

_ sen - sa - tion - al, you _ sen - sa - tion - al, Mame, mame,

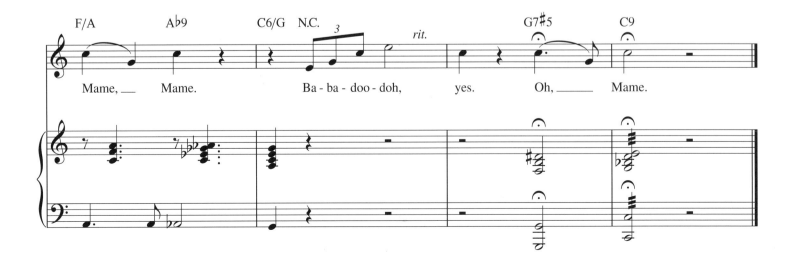

Mame, _ Mame. Ba - ba - doo - doh, yes. Oh, _____ Mame.

ON THE SUNNY SIDE OF THE STREET

Lyric by DOROTHY FIELDS
Music by JIMMY McHUGH

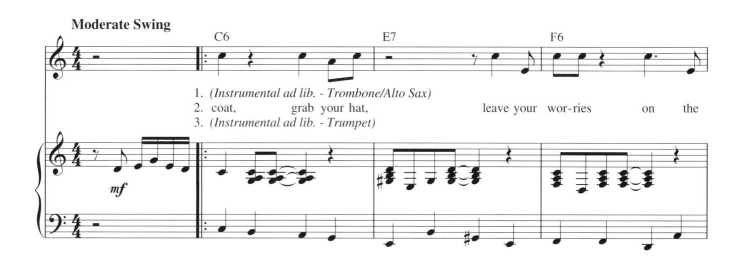

1. *(Instrumental ad lib. - Trombone/Alto Sax)*
2. coat, grab your hat, leave your wor-ries on the
3. *(Instrumental ad lib. - Trumpet)*

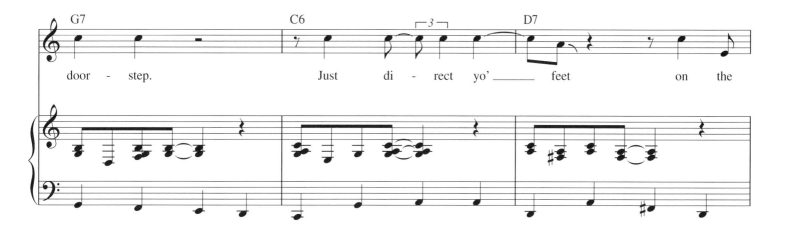

door-step. Just di - rect yo' _____ feet on the

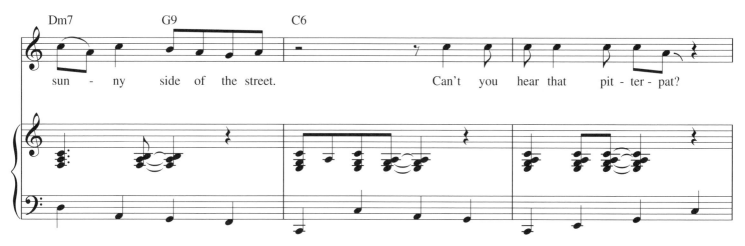

sun - ny side of the street. Can't you hear that pit - ter - pat?

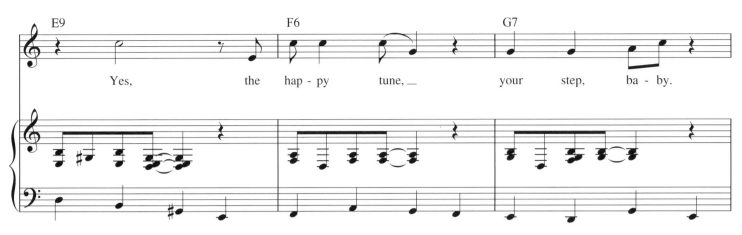

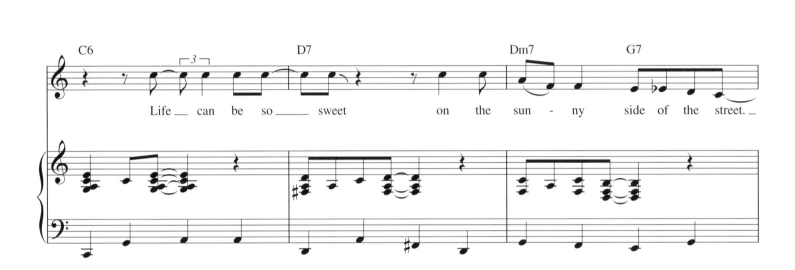

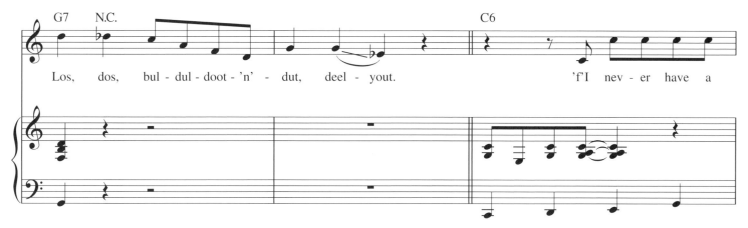

Los, dos, bul - dul - doot - 'n' - dut, deel - yout. 'f'I nev - er have a

cent, I'll be rich as "Rock - y - fel - ler," no, suh.

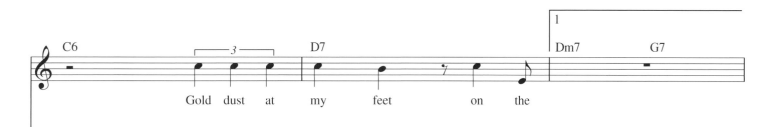

Gold dust at my feet on the

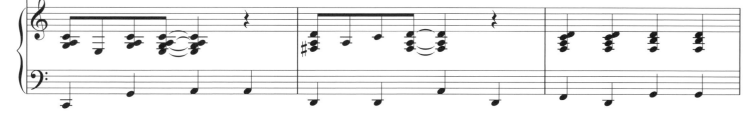

1

2

Boy,_ grab yo' sun - ny side of the street._

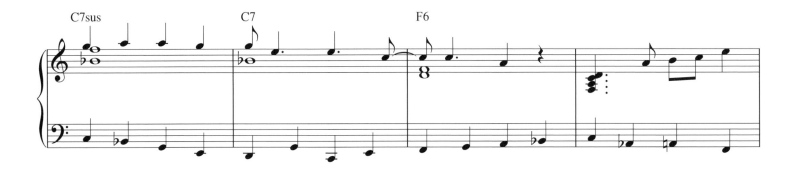

ST. LOUIS BLUES

Words and Music by
W.C. HANDY

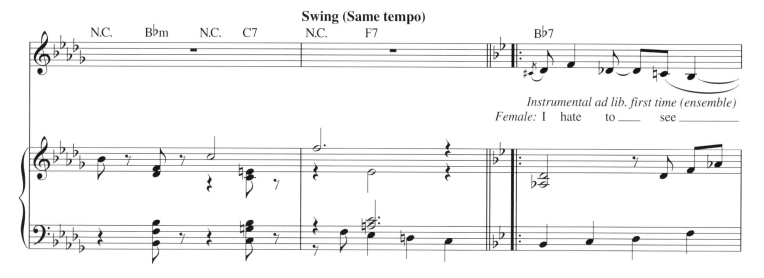

Instrumental ad lib. first time (ensemble)
Female: I hate to ___ see ___

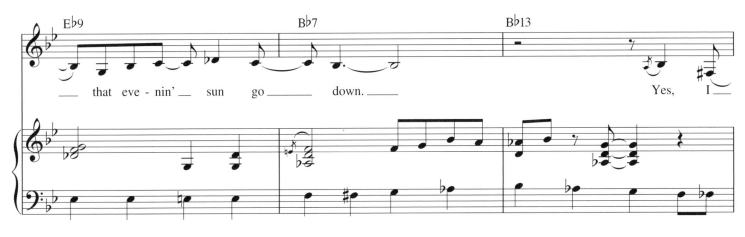

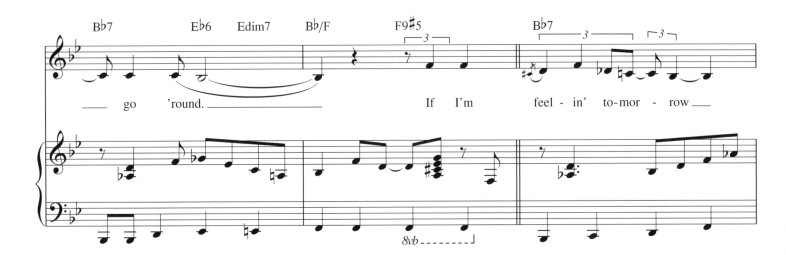

like I ___ feel ___ to - day, ___   yes, _____ feel -

- in' ___ to-mor - row ___ like I ___ feel to - day, ___

I'm ___ gon - na pack my ___ trunk and ___ make ___ my ___ get -

Rhumba

a - way. _____ 'Said Saint _____ Lou - ie wom - an,

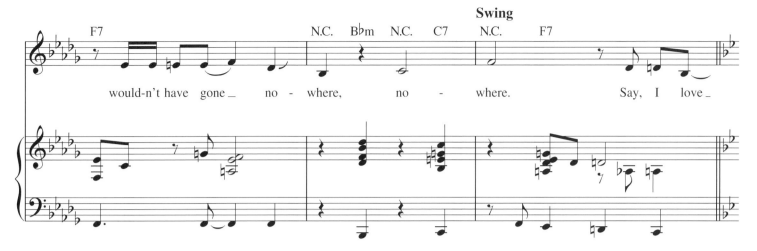

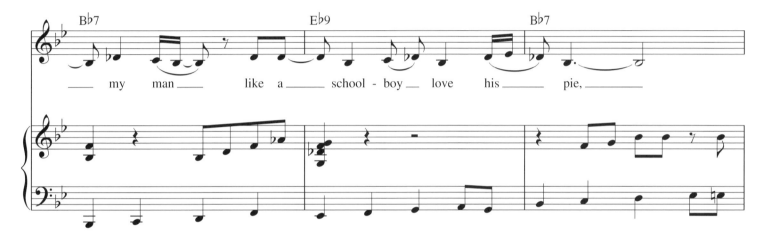

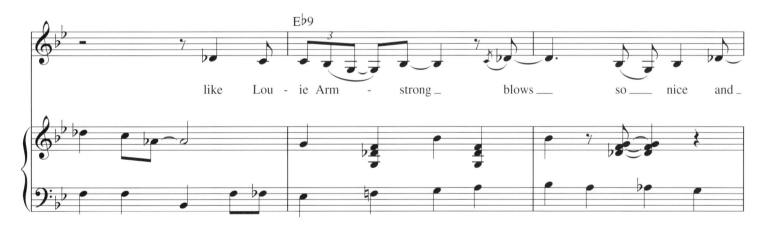

un - til the day _ I die. _

Male: Look here, ba - by!

Yes, I been to the gyp - sy ___ to get my for - tune told, ___

Instrumental ad lib. on repeat (Clarinet)

yes, ___ I been to the gyp - sy

to get my ___ for - tune told, ___ be - cause the

gyp - sy know,   'cra - zy 'bout my ___ jel - ly roll, ___   yes,

yes.   And when I went to the gyp - sy, she had   for - tunes all o - ver the place,

I'm tell - in' you. _   Yes,   the gyp - sy had ___

for - tunes all _____ o - ver the place, ___   hmm, hmm, hmm.   But when she

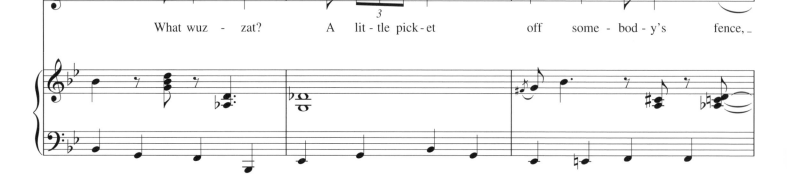

ha, ha, ha, ha! I'm gon - na whup you all o - ver your big head un -

til you learn some sense, ha, ha, ha! Take it, Trum-my, take it!

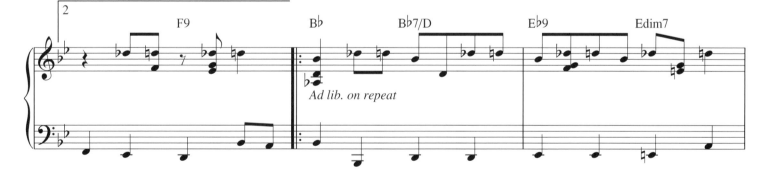

Ad lib. on repeat

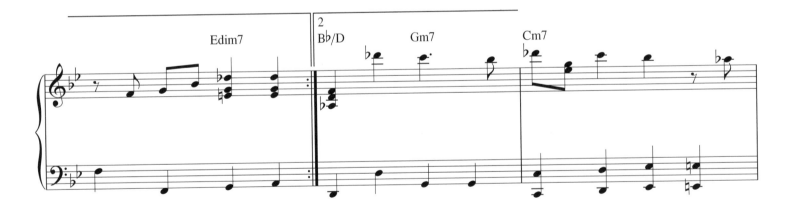

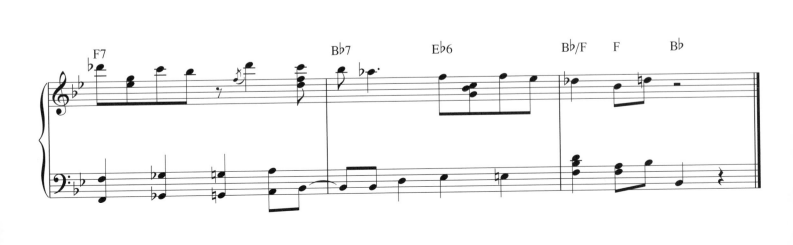

WHAT A WONDERFUL WORLD

Words and Music by GEORGE DAVID WEISS
and BOB THIELE

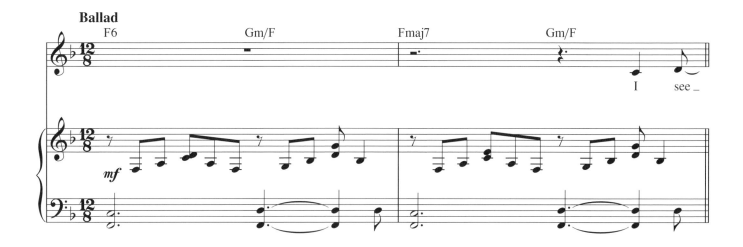

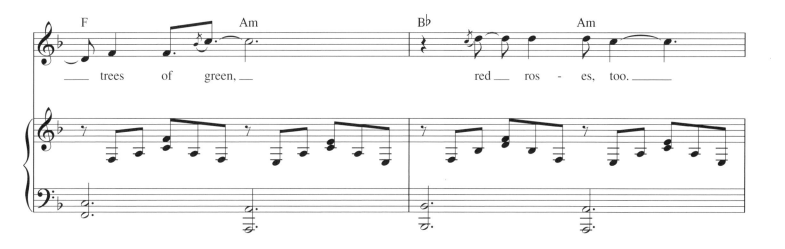

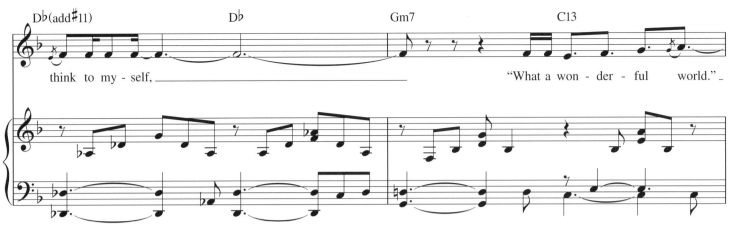

think to my-self, _____ "What a won - der - ful world." _

_____ I see

skies of blue ___ and clouds _ of white,

the bright bless-ed day, _____ the dark, _ sa-cred night, _

and I think to my-self, __ "What a won-der-ful world." __

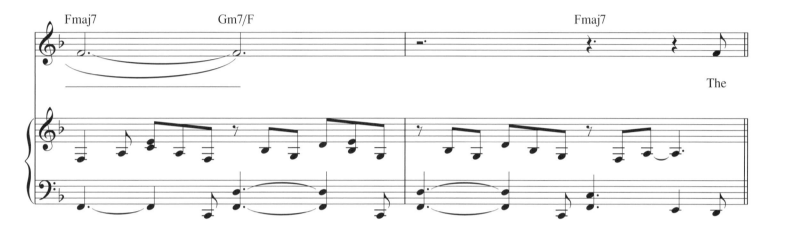

The

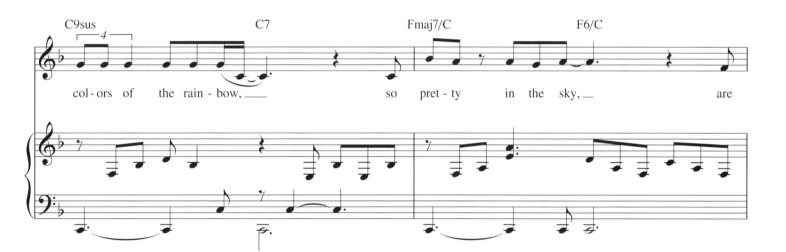

col-ors of the rain-bow, ____ so pret-ty in the sky, __ are

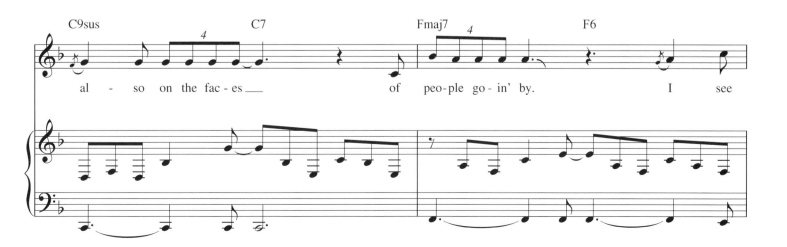

al - so on the fac-es ___ of peo-ple go-in' by. I see

friends shak - in' hands, ___ say - in', "How do you do?" ___

They're ___ real - ly say - in', ___ "I ___ love you." ___ I

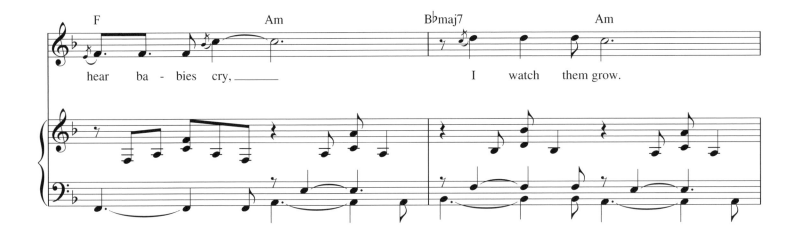

hear ba - bies cry, ___ I watch them grow.

They'll learn much more than I'll ___ ev - er know, and

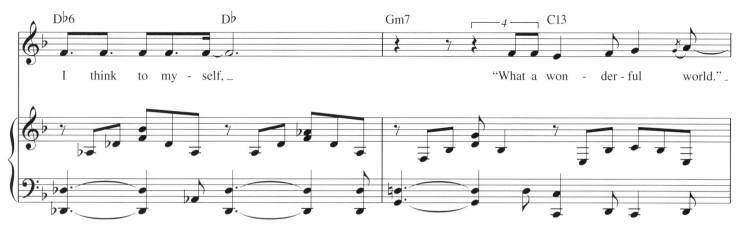

I think to my - self, _ "What a won - der - ful world." _

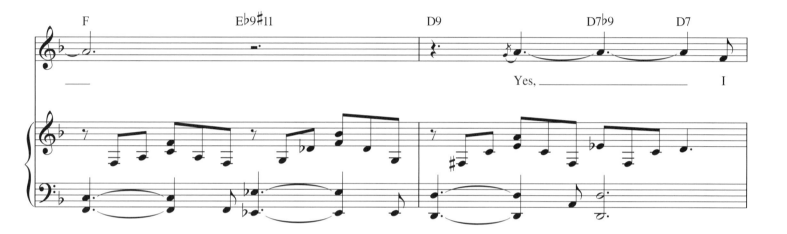

_ Yes, _____ I

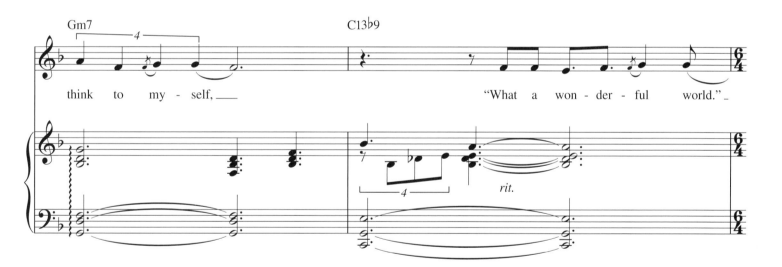

think to my - self, ___ "What a won - der - ful world." _

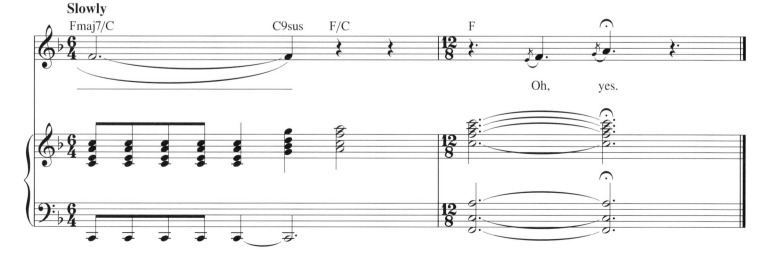

Slowly

Oh, yes.

WHEN IT'S SLEEPY TIME DOWN SOUTH

Words and Music by CLARENCE MUSE,
OTIS RENE and LEON RENE

Bright Swing

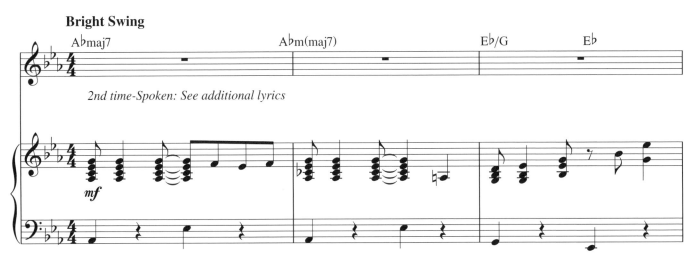

2nd time-Spoken: See additional lyrics

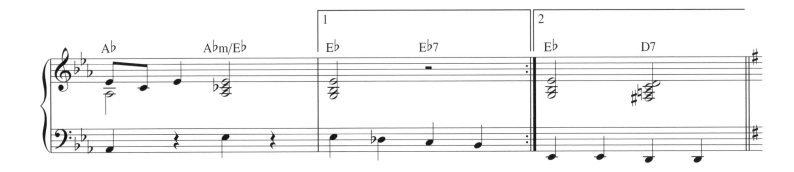

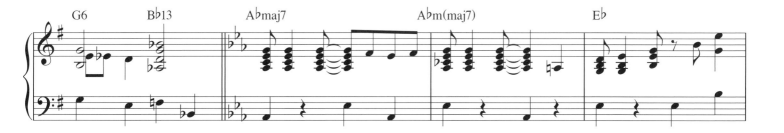

Moderately Slow

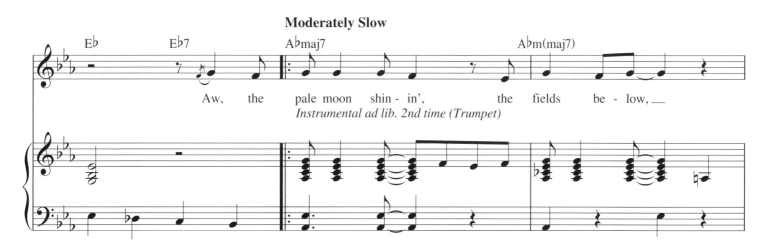

Aw, the pale moon shin-in', the fields be-low,__

Instrumental ad lib. 2nd time (Trumpet)

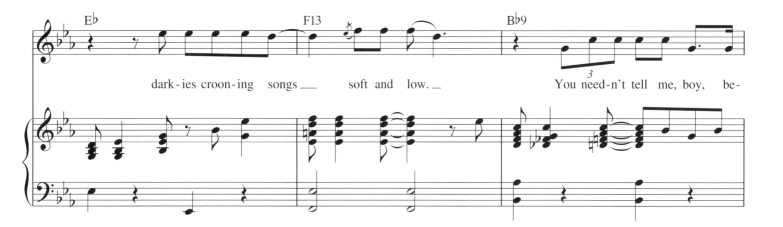

dark-ies croon-ing songs __ soft and low. __ You need-n't tell me, boy, be-

cause I know ___ it's sleep-y time ___ down south, mmm. ___

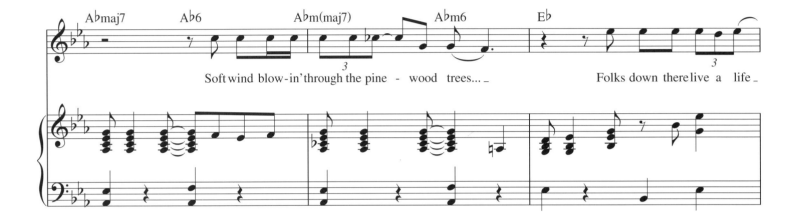

Soft wind blow-in' through the pine - wood trees... ___ Folks down there live a life ___

___ of ease. ___ When old Mam-my falls _____ up - on her knees _

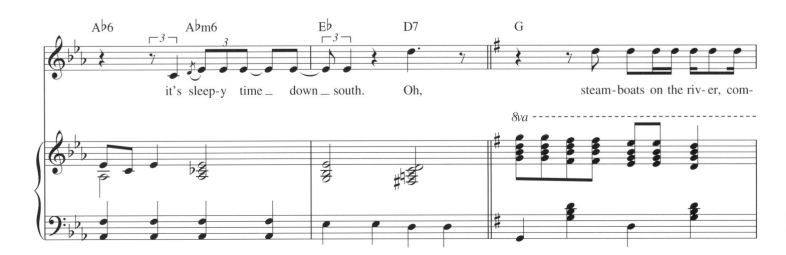

it's sleep-y time ___ down ___ south. Oh, steam-boats on the riv- er, com-

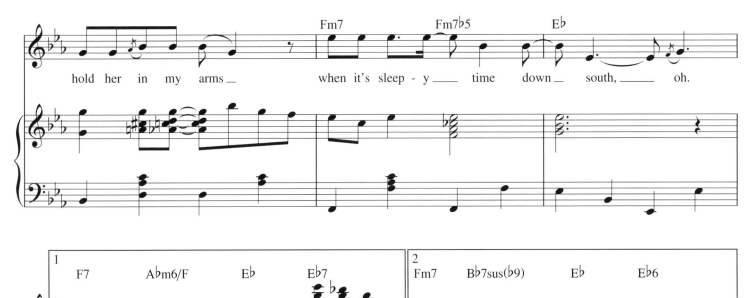

hold her in my arms __ when it's sleep - y __ time down __ south, _____ oh.

Additional lyrics

Louis:
There's a guy comin' up the street,
Look like he's from my hometown.
Look like old Charlie Alexander, man.
Well, oh, lo-lop, blop, bleep-be-deep, bop!
Well, what you say, Gate?

Charlie:
Well, what you say, Dipper?

Louis:
Well, what you know, Jim?

Charlie:
Oh, nothin' much, boy.

Louis:
How long you been up here, boy?

Charlie:
Oh, I been up here about—about a year and a half.

Louis:
A year and a half? Well man, I been up here a
long time myself. I'm goin' back home.

Charlie:
Well, go on, then!

Louis:
Aw, I'm goin'! Get some o' them red beans and...
pig ears, cabbage. You remember them sweet potato
patches? Get a load of this. This 'why I'm goin' back.

WHEN THE SAINTS GO MARCHING IN

Words by KATHERINE E. PURVIS
Music by JAMES M. BLACK

Bright Swing

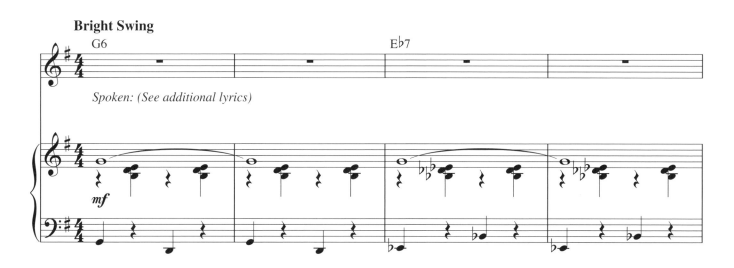

Spoken: (See additional lyrics)

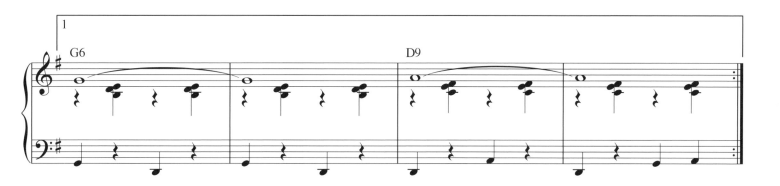

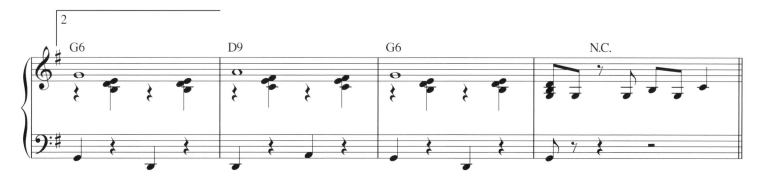

Instrumental ad lib. (Trombone)

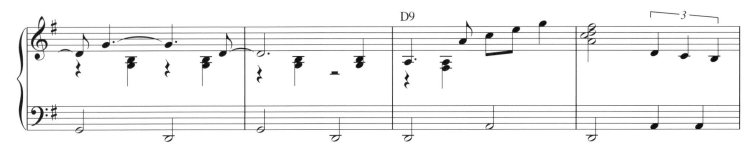

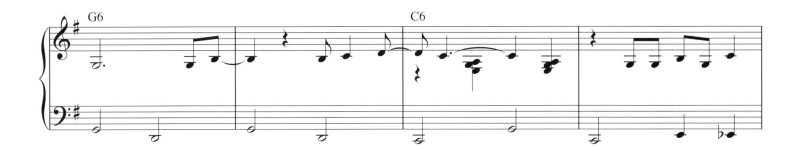

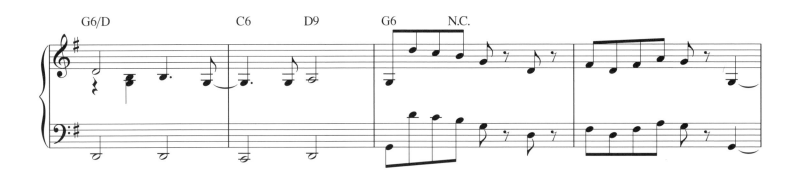

Oh,   when the

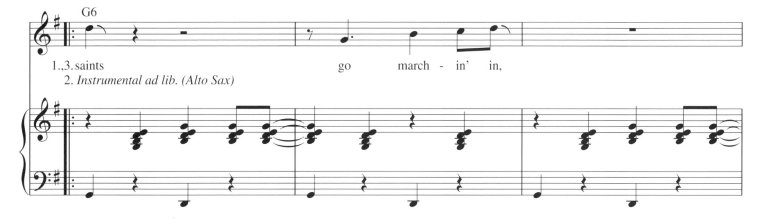

1.,3. saints go march - in' in,
2. *Instrumental ad lib. (Alto Sax)*

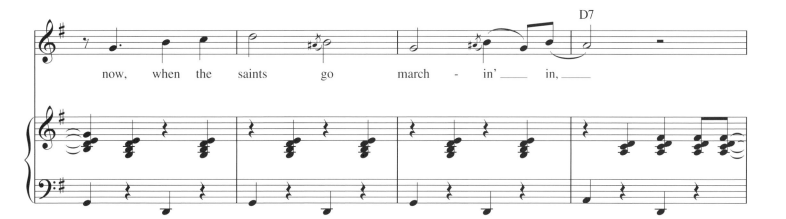

now, when the saints go march - in' in,

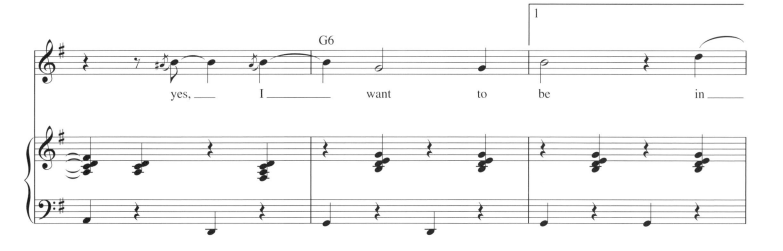

yes, I want to be in

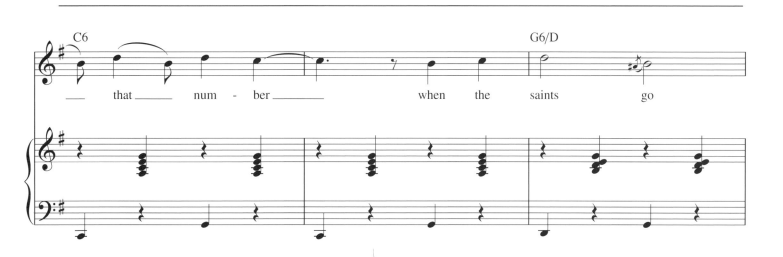

that num - ber when the saints go

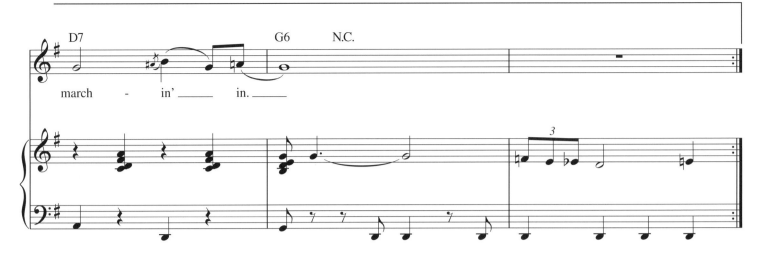

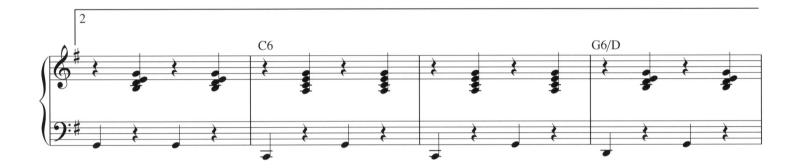

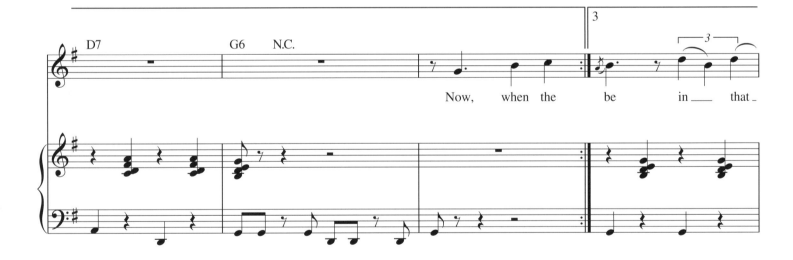

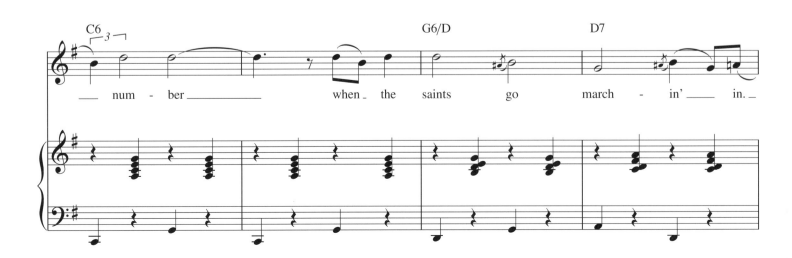

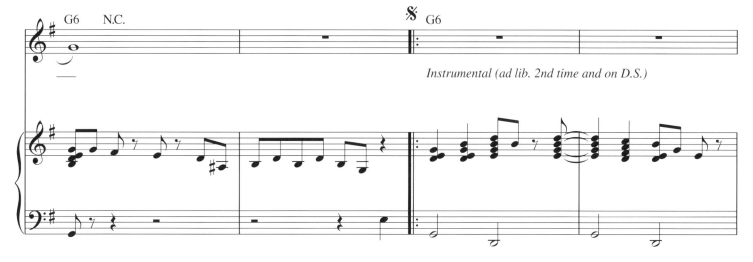

Instrumental (ad lib. 2nd time and on D.S.)

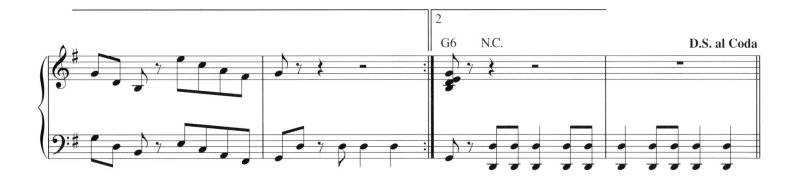

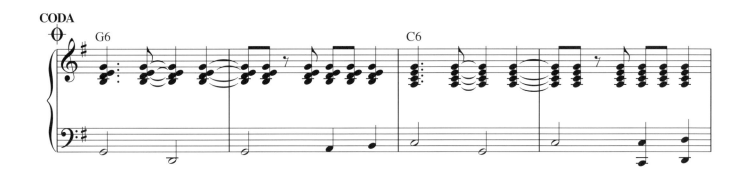

Additional Lyrics

Spoken: Sisters and Brothers, this is Reverend Satchmo
Gettin' ready to beat out this mellow sermon for ya.
My text this evenin': "When the Saints Go Marchin' In."
Here come brother Higgenbottom down the aisle
With his "trambone." Blow it, boy.

ZIP-A-DEE-DOO-DAH
from Walt Disney's SONG OF THE SOUTH

Words by RAY GILBERT
Music by ALLIE WRUBEL

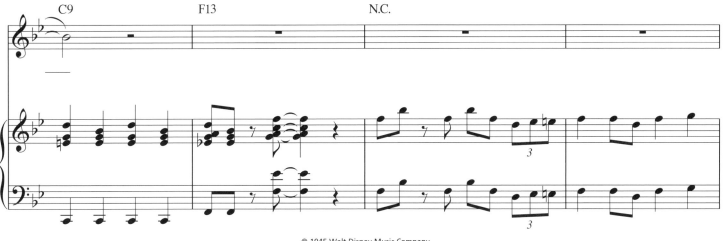

Yeah, __ zip - a - dee - doo -
Instrumental ad lib. on D.S. (Trumpet)

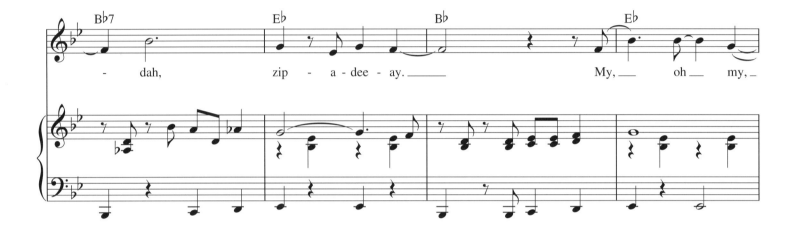

- dah, zip - a - dee - ay. _____ My, __ oh __ my, __

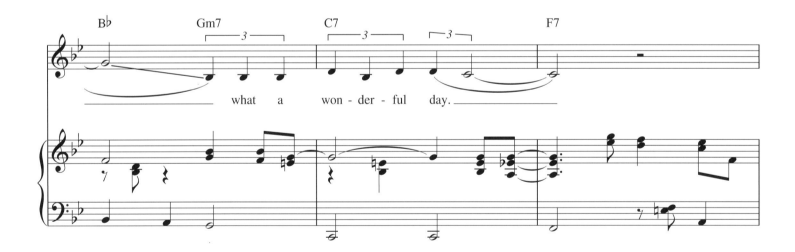

what a won - der - ful day. _____

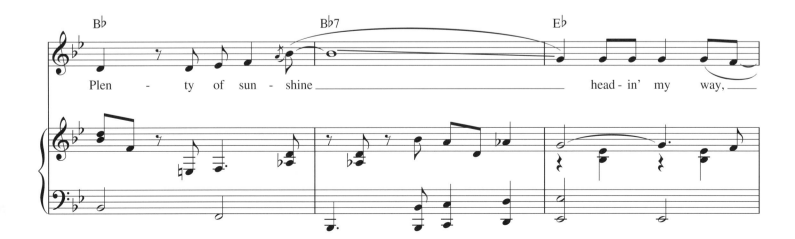

Plen - ty of sun - shine _____ head - in' my way, __

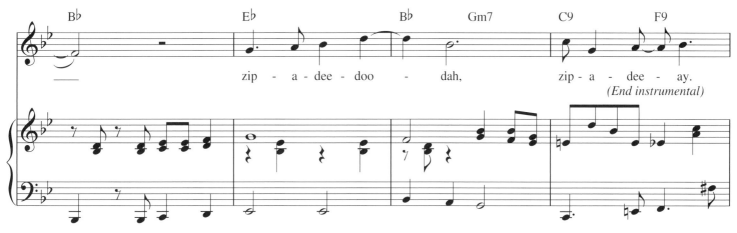

zip - a - dee - doo - dah, zip - a - dee - ay.
(End instrumental)

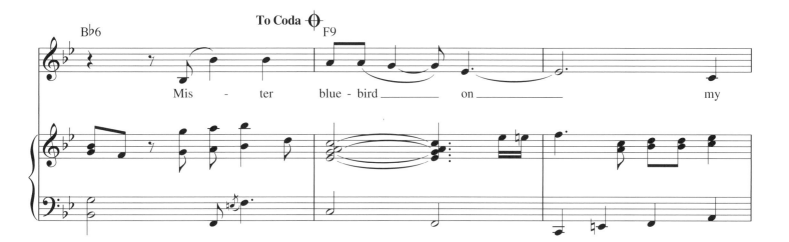

Mis - ter blue - bird ___ on ___ my

shoul - der, ___ it's the truth, it's

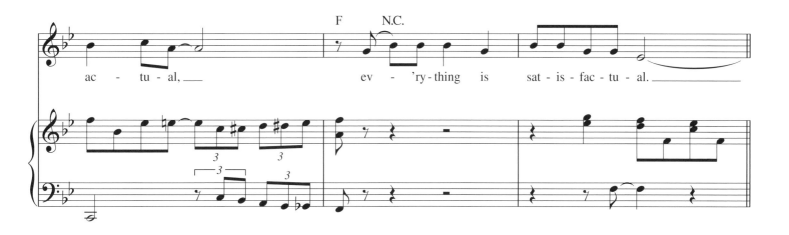

ac - tu - al, ___ ev - 'ry - thing is sat - is - fac - tu - al. ___

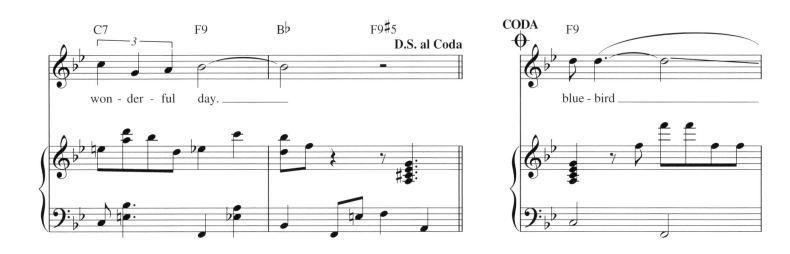

truth, it's ac - tu - al, _____ just lis-ten to the old __ Satch-

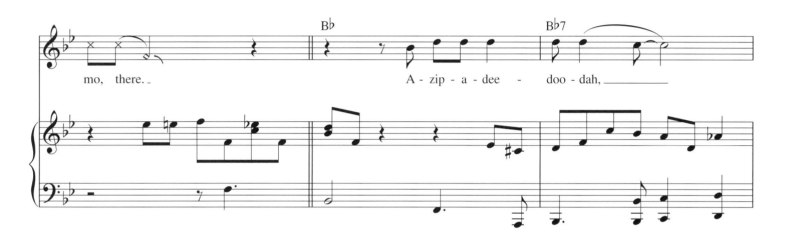

mo, there. __ A - zip - a - dee - doo - dah, _____

zip - a - dee - ay. _____ Won - der - ful

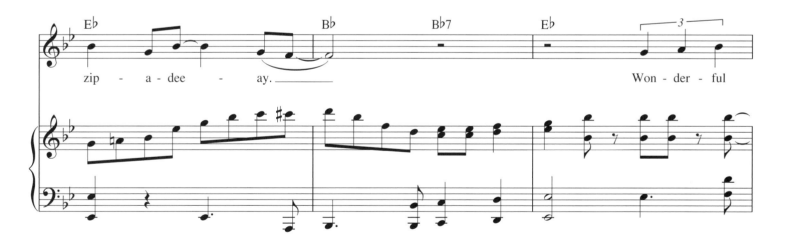

feel - in', _____ mmm, _____ won-der - ful __ day, yeah.

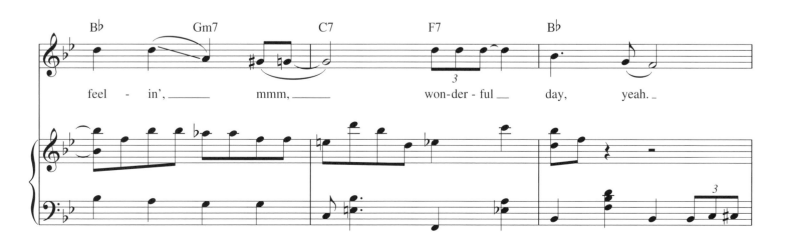